Microlig

Affordable Aviation

MICROLIGHTING
AFFORDABLE AVIATION

Chris Finnigan

CROWOOD

First published in 2001 by
The Crowood Press Ltd
Ramsbury, Marlborough
Wiltshire SN8 2HR

British Library Cataloguing-in-Publication Data
A catalogue record for this book is available from the British
Library.

ISBN 1 86126 412 7

Illustration Acknowledgements
Many thanks to the following for supplying the pictures used in
this book: Derek Allen, David Bremner, David Bremner/Pagefast
Archive, Bombardier-Rotax GMBH/Pagefast Archive, Norman
Burr, William Byrne, Chris Finnigan, Flylight Airsports Ltd, Full
Lotus Manufacturing Inc., Garmin (Europe) Ltd, Kevin Hoare,
Dr Christopher Holden, ICOM UK Ltd, Marie Jeffrey/Australian
Ultralight Federation, Judy Leden, Lynx Avionics Ltd, Brian
Milton, Pagefast Archive, Steve Percy/Pagefast Archive, Mac
Smith, Adrian Thornton Skycam Photography.

Line drawings by Keith Field.

Typeset by Jean Cussons Typesetting, Diss, Norfolk.
Printed and bound in Great Britain by Antony Rowe, Chippenham.

Contents

Foreword

At the start of the third millennium, one-third of all the aircraft registered in Britain are microlights. In the year 2005, microlights will represent half of all British-registered aircraft. Simple, easy to fly, slow and, therefore, safer than more conventional aircraft, microlights are the future. It's a *Chariots of Fire* era, in which there are still great flights to be made for those with the necessary imagination and courage.

The USA, France and Germany may currently have more microlights than Britain, but the British are well known for making big flights, some of which are featured here. American microlight (they use the term 'ultralight') pilots tend not to stray much from their own huge country, but Europeans may be seen roaming the skies all over the world. In 1992, one great European pilot, Frenchman Guy Delage, flew non-stop across the South Atlantic – 2,100km (1,350 miles) – in 26 hours. (A holy lunatic if ever there was one, he later became the first man to swim the Atlantic.)

There are still plenty of other adventures to be had. Microlight pilots are looking at the records set by early mainstream aviators, and attempting to beat them in their own small, slow craft. This, the New Aviation, is a return to a more heroic kind of flying, in which the individual is more important than the technology. Flying the English Channel, for example, still evokes the commitment that must have been made by Louis Blériot on the first such flight in 1909. Nothing quite equals that existential moment when you realize you cannot make it back to shore on a glide if the engine fails. You set off in an exalted state of mind. I have crossed thousands of miles of ocean in a microlight, but I still get a frisson of fear at the Channel crossing. I thoroughly recommend the experience; as a rite of passage, it's not unlike losing your virginity.

Chris Finnigan came to microlighting via the British Army. He was an energetic lieutenant-colonel before being snaffled to run the British Microlight Aircraft Association, and his insight and commitment prove that his appointment was a wise one. With his help, the association strives to escape from the stifling regulations that seem to have settled on general aviation. Microlighting is the future of private flying; flyers with any romance in their soul should be part of it.

Chris wrote this book in his first eighteen months at the BMAA, in order to develop his knowledge of the sport and to help promote it. Read it, and find out what microlighting has to offer.

Brian Milton
Adventurer; globe-circling and record-breaking microlight pilot

Acknowledgements

When I considered retiring early from the British Army to become the Chief Executive of the British Microlight Aircraft Association, I had to think carefully about my decision. I had been taught to fly Chipmunks on the Army pilot's course and had a passion for flying that was beyond doubt. Microlighting had provided me with an affordable way to keep my flying up and, indeed, to improve my abilities as a pilot.

The Army had been good to me and I had reached a comfortable rank, but job satisfaction was declining, as I became more desk-bound, and eighteen house moves in twenty years of marriage were just too many. The BMAA post provided the answer.

I have been delighted by the warmth and support given by the British microlighting movement. Microlighters have been generous with their advice and time and, even though they don't always agree with the way things are being done, most will listen and take a considered view. Microlight clubs always offer a warm welcome, hot tea or coffee, and enthusiastic and passionate conversation.

I am indebted to those who have helped me in the preparation of this book. Adventurer Brian Milton, the first man to fly around the world in a microlight, and also a journalist, TV presenter, highly skilled pilot and all-round 'good egg', kindly wrote the foreword and gave freely of his time to advise me on its content and on the history of microlighting. Brian Cosgrove, the first Chief Executive of the BMAA, and the man who has done more than most to bring respectability to micro-lighting in the eyes of the British CAA, read the first chapter and encouraged me to continue. Norman Burr of Pagefast Limited, publishers of *Microlight Flying* (and other excellent aviation publications), allowed me to plunder his photograph archives and identified some of the more obscure earlier machines.

Thanks are also due to Lynn Benson and Eden Blyth, who have done such good work on the BMAA website, including the superb history section, which I used extensively in my research; to my aeronautical engineer colleague Guy Gratton, BMAA Chief Technical Officer, who made sure my technical explanations were correct; and to Chris Draper of Medway Microlights whose website provided me with most of my research material on Eppo Numan.

I am grateful to the many keen micro-lighting photographers who have kindly allowed me to use their work with just a simple picture credit.

Finally, my thanks and gratitude are due to all the microlighters I have met wherever I have flown in the UK, and elsewhere. Their comradeship, friendliness, practical help and technical advice – to me and to each other – are products of an enthusiasm and passion for their sport that are found in few other activities.

Whoever you are, wherever you are and whatever you fly, I wish you clear skies, gentle breezes and soft landings always.

Chris Finnigan

NOTES

'Microlight' is the internationally accepted term used to describe an ultra-light aircraft below a certain total weight (*see* Chapter 2 for more on the definition). The term 'ultra-light' or 'ULM' is still used in many countries to describe such aircraft.

Throughout this book, I have included features on pilots who are, in my view, worthy of the accolade of 'microlight hero' or 'heroine'. Inevitably, the selection has been subjective and many have been left out. These include outstanding British competition pilots such as Paul Dewhurst and Simon Baker (both multiple world champions), and other pilots who have made remarkable flights, such as Ben Ashman, who flew with Judy Leden to Jordan, David Young, who flew around Africa with Christina Dodwell, Storm Smith and Rory Jeffes, who flew from India to UK, James Edmonds, who flew from England to Beijing and the Frenchmen Lafitte and Delage, to name but a few. Perhaps one day all microlighting's inspiring stories will appear in a book of their own.

1 Welcome to the World of Microlighting

INTRODUCTION

Flight has been the dream of man since he first saw birds wheeling in the skies above his primitive, earthbound existence. The sheer joy and exhilaration of taking to the air in control of your own aircraft cannot be fully appreciated by those who have not experienced it. Those who fly are different; even when their feet are firmly on the ground, their eyes keep turning to the sky, assessing the weather and longing for their next flight.

This book will take you into the world of microlighting, where affordable aviation for all is a reality. It will explain how microlights came about and how, through microlighting, ordinary men and women (and not just the rich, well-connected or highly talented) can reach for the sky as pilots of their own aircraft.

From its earliest beginnings – from designs on the drawing boards of visionaries such as Leonardo da Vinci, through tower jumping (which was usually fatal), balloons, gliders and airships – manned aviation was initially slow to progress. Once aviation became a reality, the pace of its progress picked up rapidly. Throughout the twentieth century aviation developed faster than almost any other technological advance made by mankind. To go from leaving the ground in powered, heavier-than-air machines to breaking free from Planet Earth and advancing into space in such a short period of history is indeed remarkable.

The most significant aviation milestone was the first powered flight, made by the legendary Wright Brothers in December 1903 at Kittyhawk, North Carolina, USA. From that beginning, powered flight has evolved into today's world-shrinking global airline industry, which carries many millions into the skies each year with hardly a thought for the pioneers of flight and engineering who made it all possible. Journeys that used to take weeks and months now take a matter of hours. Soon, such journeys will take even less time as the technologies developed from man's advances into Space become accessible to the travelling public. Air travel for everyone, not just military pilots, astronauts and the privileged few who can afford to fly on Concorde, will no longer be at subsonic speeds, but will push well beyond the sound barrier by reaching outside the Earth's atmosphere into Space.

Prior to the advent of microlight aircraft, access to personal or private aviation was not widely available. It remained for a long time the preserve of the wealthy few with both the money and the time to indulge in what was initially a very risky activity. The first people to be paid for flying were military pilots, for whom the risks of aviation were part of the wider dangers of warfare. As time has passed, flying has become more technologically sophisticated – and commensurately safer. Government regulation of flying introduced airworthiness requirements, obliging aeroplanes and their engines to meet exacting standards for safety reasons. While reducing the number of accidents, this caused the cost of manufacturing aeroplanes to rise. When mandatory maintenance schedules (to be carried out only by licensed engineers) were introduced, the cost of owning a private aeroplane went up again. The requirement for some blind flying instruments and radio navigation and communication equipment, known collectively as avionics, added to the spiralling costs. Private flying was soon beyond the financial reach of the average person.

Some of those who managed to scrape together the money to pay for Private Pilot's Licence training went on to become professional pilots. Many more struggled to maintain enough flying hours in their log books to keep their licences current, before eventually having to give up their impossibly expensive hobby.

In the years after the Second World War, a typical flying club, particularly in Britain, became a class- and status-conscious institution. It tends to be dominated by retired military aviators, keeping their hand in as instructors, and those few people who have the means to rent or own and maintain a small aeroplane. The younger instructor is usually an 'hour-builder', being paid a nominal wage for the privilege of increasing his or her flying hours by teaching others to fly. Having accumulated sufficient hours, he or she moves on down the route to qualifying as a professional pilot on the flight deck of a modern airliner. Many such instructors are talented individuals, but their professional goals sometimes conflict with their teaching performance.

The unpredictability of the British weather, ever-increasing costs, an elitist atmosphere in clubs and some indifferent instructors meant that many aspiring private pilots in Britain either give up before obtaining a licence, or drop out of flying within a couple of years because they cannot afford to continue developing their skills.

PHILOSOPHY OF MICROLIGHTING

Anyone who has been bitten by the flying bug will understand the agony of having to give it up. Flying is not so much a hobby as a consuming passion. The sense of achievement and the sheer exhilaration experienced by those taking to the air on their own for the first time is a lifelong memory. Before microlights came on the scene, many people longed for the experience, but simply could not afford it. Private Pilot's Licence holders could not afford to continue flying. Many formed groups or syndicates to share the expenses of aeroplane ownership, but costs were still relatively high and demand was high whenever the weather was suitable.

They all needed an affordable and simple way of flying for fun. The solution would have to be minimal in terms of construction and engine, simple enough to control that it might be flown by pilots of modest ability, and easily maintained by the owner, preferably at home in a garage or shed. The early flexwing trike (*see* photo on page 11) probably represents the simplest form of microlight, apart from foot-launched machines.

The concept of simplicity and affordability has been the driving force behind the microlight movement. It has created a common bond between people from all walks of life, and allows many flying fanatics to earn a meagre but intensely satisfying living by teaching others. The movement also supports a small but innovative industry producing microlight aircraft in complete or kit form. Today, whenever the weather is right, men and women gather at airfields, small airstrips and farmers' fields. They share their experiences and learn from each other about flying, navigation and aircraft

An early and simple flexwing microlight.

maintenance, but mostly they are there to fly.

A BRIEF HISTORY

Microlighting has developed as a sport from the two distinct origins of hang-gliding and conventional aeroplanes. Broadly speaking, flexwing microlights developed from hang-gliders, while the three-axis microlight has adapted conventional aircraft design.

Flexwing Microlights

In 1948, the delta flexwing was patented as the Rogallo wing. It was conceived and designed by American aeronautical engineer Francis Rogallo, who had been working on a research project into low-speed flight. The design was a departure from conven-tional wisdom, which had dictated that all aircraft wings should be rigid. The flexwing developed further in the early 1960s, when Rogallo was involved in studying ways of recovering space vehicles to Earth. He thought of using a flexwing as a way of deploying a controllable wing system to steer space capsules back to the ground, rather than just letting them drift down under a parachute.

The US military commissioned a series of trials in which motors of increasing size and power were mated to Rogallo wings, to examine the many potential uses for powered flexwing aircraft. The possibilities included pilotless aerial reconnaissance, an aerial freight carriage system to be towed by helicopter, and a form of steerable para-chute for the covert insertion of special forces troops and to allow combat pilots who

11

had ejected from their aircraft to steer themselves away from enemy lines.

While the flexwing never caught on for these military applications, it did attract the attention of those with less serious activities in mind. In the early 1960s, in California, a man named Barry Palmer began building Rogallo flexwings for fun flying. By the end of the decade he had progressed to attaching first chainsaw motors then snow-mobile engines to them. The engine power was limited and the Rogallo wing was still underdeveloped, however, and for the time being his invention went no further.

The next stage in the development of the flexwing came from water-skiing. Seeking a more exciting sensation of flight than they were getting from jumping ramps, French water-skiers had attached themselves to kite-like wings. When towed behind a powerful speedboat, the skier could be lifted into the air for as long as the boat driver would allow. Australian John Dickinson knew about the disappointing Rogallo wing trials and decided to go one better than the French water-skiers. He adapted a Rogallo wing for use with water skis, adding a triangular control frame (now known as an A-frame), which allowed the wing to be steered and controlled in pitch.

In 1969, Dickinson's friend Bill Moyes, an international standard Australian water-skier, took this wing to the world water-skiing championships in Copenhagen. He demonstrated its capabilities by releasing the tow from the speedboat after he had risen to a good height and gliding down to make a controlled landing on the water. The demonstration was repeated in the USA by Moyes' partner Bill Bennett, first at the US water-skiing championships in Berkeley, California, and then in a spectacular flight off New York's Manhattan Island, where he landed, after a lengthy glide, safely on the water at the feet of the Statue of Liberty.

Bernard Danis, the original French kite water-skier, took the new concept back to France and, with friends Jean-François Moveau and Christian Raisin, transformed it into hang-gliding. On the edge of the French Alps, the trio made the first hang-glider flights from the hills above the lake at Annecy, suspended under a flexwing using an A-frame control system. At the same time, in Southern California, 'bamboo butterflies' were being built by Jack Lambie, Richard Millar and Paul McReady and other friends, and flown from the top of sand dunes. On 23 May 1971 one of these 'butterflies' flew over 196ft in a flight lasting 11 seconds, and hang-gliding was born. Appropriately, this was the hundredth anniversary of the birth of Otto Lilienthal, the German aviation pioneer who experimented with footlaunched gliders and made over 2,000 flights before he was killed testing a wing in 1896; Lilienthal is seen by many as the spiritual 'father' of the New Aviation of hang-gliding and microlighting.

The sport of hang-gliding progressed rapidly, despite a number of fatal accidents and many more resulting in serious injury, until it reached the point at which sound and well-designed hang-gliders were being manufactured and sold. People also started to think about offering training, so that newcomers to the sport did not have to follow the same, often painful, route as the pioneers.

Hang-glider pilots living in the mountains or close to high cliffs or hills found it relatively easy to launch themselves into flight. For those who lived in flatter regions, however, the journey to a suitable launch site was often a costly and time-consuming affair, with the added risk that the weather might have changed by the time of arrival.

It was not long before hang-glider pilots began experimenting again with motors. In the early 1970s, a number of motorized hang-glider designs began to emerge in

Europe and the USA. One involved a 'backpack'-style motor, to be worn by the pilot, who would be suspended under a Rogallo-type flexwing, just like any other hang-glider pilot. It proved to be less than efficient – the pilot's body shielded much of the 'pusher' propeller from a clean airflow – and also put unwanted weight on the pilot's body in the event of a heavy landing.

Another method mounted the engine on the keel of the flexwing. The small engines used would produce just about enough power to keep a flexwing aloft. However, it was not powerful enough for a take-off from flat ground and a climb to height.

The most successful designs put the engine on a 'trike' unit. This had the advantages not only of keeping weight off the pilot's body but also put the weight of both

The Cosmos Dragster 25, c.1985, shows the simple construction of the basic trike.

motor and wing on wheels (*see* photo on page 11). The trike allowed a much easier and more dignified take-off than the alternative, which involved the pilot running at full tilt into wind while carrying the entire weight of the aircraft.

Many pilots and engineers were thinking along the same lines at the same time, but Frenchman Roland Magallon is generally credited as the inventor of the trike. He went on to produce and market his design, and according to some he did for the trike what Henry Ford had done for the motor car.

The flexwing microlight had arrived!

THREE-AXIS MICROLIGHTS

As flexwing microlights were being developed, the three-axis microlight was also evolving. While Europe was focused on flexwings, the Australians and Americans were either motorizing fixed-wing hang-gliders or producing simple aircraft specifically designed for power that owed their characteristics to conventional aeroplane design. Conventional aeroplanes were of either bi-plane (two wings one above the other) or monoplane (one single wing) construction. During the First World War tri-planes had been built – the most famous was the Fokker Triplane fighter used by German ace Manfred von Richthofen, more commonly known as the 'Red Baron' – but this design, described by some as a flying 'venetian blind', soon lost favour.

Three-axis microlights have a control system that allows the pilot to control the aircraft in the three axes of pitch, roll and yaw. The flexwing microlight has just two axes of control – pitch and roll. (For more on the different control systems and the principles of flight that govern their use, *see* Chapter 2.)

While the flexwing was a departure from conventional wisdom, three-axis microlight development worked on the principle of making conventional aeroplanes lighter and simpler. Tube and fabric construction methods were used. Light but strong aluminium alloys provided the material for the tubes, and synthetic Dacron fabric soon replaced the cotton and dope that had been used for coverings.

Different wing configurations were used in three-axis designs. 'Flying wings', seen on the Icarus V and B-10 Mitchell Wing designs, involved a single wing with vertical control surfaces incorporated as tip rudders or winglets. Aircraft with separate tail-control surfaces included bi-planes such as the Easy Riser and monoplanes such as the famous Quicksilver, created in 1972 by Bob Lovejoy. The Quicksilver evolved from a fixed-wing hang-glider and was designed from the outset to have a tail. This meant that it was a relatively easy task to convert it into a fairly conventional-looking ultra-light aircraft. The Quicksilver sold in its thousands, setting the standard for a simple tube and single-surface fabric construction with a trike-style undercarriage, and was imitated many times.

In the early days, the development of the three-axis microlight claimed its share of victims, as pioneers were killed test-flying new designs. By the late 1970s, ultralight aviation had really 'taken off' in the USA, as machines like John Chotia's Weedhopper came to prominence with a large-scale production run. This two-axis fixed-wing design was the origin of many of the three-axis microlights being flown today. John Chotia achieved so much for the sport of microlighting but, tragically, paid the ultimate price for his achievements; he was killed in 1981 test-flying one of his own machines.

The Pathfinder, c. 1982, is a good example of the tube and fabric construction of the early three-axis machine.

A British-registered example of the Weedhopper.

In 1979, the American Aerolights company began producing the Eagle in the USA. Designed as a canard aeroplane, with a smaller wing out in front of the main wing, it was a safe and easy-to-handle beginners' machine. It sold very well in its home market and made a significant impact in the UK in 1980, when it was shown to microlighters by British pilot Gerry Breen. Dave Garrison and Paul Baker had introduced two Pterodactyl Ptledges to the UK at the end of 1979 and were soon importing kits and selling complete aircraft. There was a great rush of interest in the American three-axis machines from those who were more comfortable with a fixed-wing design. These customers wanted to fly cheaply, but not in a flexwing, which some saw as an overgrown hang-glider.

SAFETY AND RISK

It is a sad fact that pilots have been killed during the development of microlights, so how safe is microlighting as a sport? Like all other forms of aviation, it is challenging and exciting, but microlight aircraft tend to be more forgiving of stupidity and neglect than heavier and faster aeroplanes. The risk element can never be totally eliminated but, properly managed, it can be reduced to an absolute minimum.

Today's microlight aircraft is very different from the early designs. Inevitably, trial and error were the basis for advancement, but much more is now known about the physics of very light aviation. Modern materials and construction methods have made the microlight one of the safest types of aircraft. The low weight and relatively

15

Brian Cosgrove in a Pterodactyl canard machine.

low flying speed of the microlight mean that it has low inertia – it approaches and lands much more slowly than most other types of aircraft, lands in a short distance and comes to a stop quickly.

The engines used in microlight aircraft used to have a reputation for failing frequently in flight. This may have been the case in the days when lawnmower engines and other motors not designed for aviation use were used to power microlights. Today's purpose-built two- and four-stroke engines are powerful, efficient and reliable, if operated and maintained correctly. If an engine does fail in a microlight, it is usually possible, because of the craft's light weight and low flying speed, to land safely in a field with little or no damage to the aircraft or occupants. Only the very unlucky, those who fail regularly to practise forced landings, and those who reduce their margin for error by flying too low over country where there are no big, open areas in which to land, are likely to get hurt.

The training of microlight pilots has now been properly organized in many countries, based on progressive training courses. The aim is to produce safe and competent aviators who know what they are doing, what they and their machines are capable of and, more importantly, what they are not capable of. Pilots are no longer expected to 'pick it up as they go along'. Now they can be trained in two-seat machines by professional instructors and will not be allowed to fly solo until they are ready for it.

Microlight aircraft are now subject to some form of regulation in most countries. In Britain, controlled design and production standards ensure that they are manufactured to be safe. Mandatory annual inspections mean that aircraft have to be maintained in an airworthy state before being allowed to continue to fly.

People do still have accidents in microlight aircraft. However, if the pilot has been well trained, and has used common sense in planning and carrying out their flying activities, and the machine has been kept in good condition, he or she should be able to survive an accident without serious injury, and often without any injury at all. People

A Rotax 447 two-cylinder, two-stroke, air-cooled motor.

are still killed in microlight aircraft accidents, but such events are increasingly rare and are usually due to pilot error rather than to a failure of the aircraft.

THE NEW AVIATION

Microlights are a fundamental part of the concept of 'New Aviation' – a collective term for the 'airsports' of microlighting, hang-gliding and para-gliding, and gyroplane flying. New Aviation has turned the world of private aviation upside down, providing new routes into flying and alternatives to the conventional aeroplanes of the private club or school.

Brian Milton, the first man to complete a round-the-world flight by microlight, describes the history of the New Aviation in his book *Children of the Wind*. He sees it as a return to simple, low-speed flight, a new branch of aviation that picks up from the original pioneers, developing a thrilling new activity for the ordinary recreational flyer.

In its early days, in the 1970s, micro-lighting was seen by many as a crazy new pastime for lunatics with some kind of death wish. Microlight pilots were regarded as anti-social aerial 'Hell's Angels', whose noisy machines were designed to annoy the general public. The individualistic nature of many hang-glider and microlight pilots, who were often literally taking their lives into their own hands, did little to alter this impression. Training was either by trial and error; sometimes, there was a pre-flight brief on the ground and then the pilots attempted to do the necessary in the air. Most survived their introduction to micro-lighting but, sadly, some did not.

In Britain, the number of deaths in this new and totally unregulated form of aviation led to questions being asked in Parliament. The UK Civil Aviation Authority (CAA), which controls all commercial and private aviation within the UK, was tasked to regulate microlight flying, in order to ensure a reduction in the number of deaths. Safety standards were soon drawn up and applied.

The British Minimum Aircraft Association, now the British Microlight Aircraft Association (BMAA), was formed originally to provide a focus for powered hang-glider pilots. They had been regarded as troublesome within their own British Hang Gliding Association because their machines were too noisy and soon led to complaints from the public. In 1980, the BMAA began negotiations with the CAA over the self-regulation of microlighting.

After twenty years of alternating battles and co-operation between the BMAA and the CAA, a structured sport has emerged in which the BMAA has obtained a great deal of freedom to run its own affairs for the benefit of its members. Pilot and instructor training systems have been set up, with a detailed training syllabus at each level, detailed handbooks for study and an instructor revalidation system to ensure training is to a common high standard. A nationwide network of inspectors ensures that all microlight aircraft in Britain are inspected annually to ensure that they are airworthy before revalidation of their permit.

It has been a similar story in many countries, with a gradual, sometimes difficult progression to the self-government of microlighting by members' associations. A more responsible and self-disciplined approach to the sport by its participants has largely dispelled the public view of the microlight

A high degree of skill is shown by instructor Jim Greenshields as he lands a flexwing on top of a moving truck.

Going one better: Greenshields lands a Thruster on a platform on top of a moving Mini!
(Photo: Adrian Thornton)

pilot as an anti-social lunatic. Today, microlight pilots are people from all walks of life who like flying relatively slowly, but cheaply and safely.

Occasionally, the adventurous and pioneering spirit of the early microlighters still bursts free from the confines of regulation. In 1999, a flexwing was flown under all the bridges across the River Thames in London, between Kew and Westminster, by a daring, unidentified pilot. At one point, it is alleged, the distance between the river and the underside of the bridge was as little as 8m (27ft). The flight broke a number of laws, and upset officialdom, but it did demonstrate that a skilled pilot can fly a microlight to very fine degrees of precision.

Microlight Heroes: Richard Meredith-Hardy

Richard Meredith-Hardy is an unconventional and uncompromising Englishman whose epic journey from England to South Africa in a flexwing first set the standard for long-distance microlight flights. This accomplished microlight pilot has been world champion and has held a number of microlight world records in various categories. He was also at the forefront of the introduction of foot-launched microlights into the UK and remains an enthusiastic FLM pilot and competitor.

Richard Meredith-Hardy's African adventure started on 28 August 1985, when he took to the air from London's docks area in a Mainair Gemini Flash flexwing with a Rotax 447 two-stroke engine. Ahead of him were 10,000 miles (16,000km) of flying, which would

include the first crossing of the Alps by a flexwing, the first un-refuelled flight of eight hours over water and the first desert crossing by a microlight.

After a short first leg to an overnight stop in Kent, Meredith-Hardy met up with his ground support team – John Eskdale and Nicky Lindsay-Smith, travelling in a specially modified 14-ton, 30-year-old German MAN truck loaded with spares and equipment, including a kitchen sink! The following morning he set off for Lydd, where he would refuel before flying across the English Channel, his first water crossing. Taking off from a long grass surface, he just made it into the air, clipping the fence at the end of the runway and damaging a wheel spat and the propeller; the adventure had nearly been over before it had really begun.

After refuelling at Lydd, the journey across to France was uneventful. When the support crew arrived at Calais, their pilot was nowhere to be seen. A few frantic phone calls revealed that Calais had closed for the day – due to some mix-up over the time difference – and he had had to land at Le Touquet! After a couple of days' delay, waiting for good weather, the microlight crossed the Alps, climbing to 10,000ft, giving the pilot some stunning views.

Bureaucracy became a real problem in Italy – microlights were illegal at the time. Even after a government minister in Rome was contacted for clearance to fly over the country, Meredith-Hardy was obliged to explain over and over again to incredulous local airport officials that his microlight was legal and registered in the UK, and that he was flying to South Africa in it. Landing at Italian airports was a challenge, too; on one occasion, the microlight had to approach with a large passenger jet in front and another closing rapidly from behind.

The crossing of the Adriatic Sea, from Italy to Corfu, was the first leg out of sight of land, with the long-range fuel tank coming into use. Navigation was vital here; he did not want to miss Corfu and land in Albania, at the time the most secret and isolated country in Europe. Island-hopping down the west coast of Greece, Meredith-Hardy flew on to Crete where he would refuel and make preparations for the daunting Mediterranean Sea crossing to North Africa. Approaching Crete over the sea, he was refused permission to land because of heavy air traffic caused by the summer tourist trade. When he explained that he had no fuel to go anywhere else, he was cleared to land – again, he found himself approaching in between two passenger jets.

From Crete, the intrepid pilot set off across the sea, headed for the radio beacon at El Daba in North Africa, but flying on a compass bearing until he could pick up the signal. He was well equipped, with survival equipment and inflatable airbeds inside the wing to keep the microlight afloat in the event of a ditching in the sea. As he made landfall in North Africa he had flown 410 nautical miles in just over eight hours; for four and a half of those hours he had been out of sight of land. A small two-stroke engine, not certificated for aircraft use, was all that was keeping him from a watery touch-down in a place where sharks are not unknown. The support team arrived in Africa at about the same time, despite a breakdown, and nearly missing the ferry.

North African officialdom proved to be even more problematic than in Italy, with exorbitant landing fees, even for tiny microlights. The support team also had to hand over unofficial sums of money at military checkpoints on the road to Cairo. Several days were spent in the chaos of Cairo before the necessary permissions and paperwork were obtained and the flight could proceed. Failing to get permission for the truck to leave Egypt by the Red Sea

coast, the ground crew decided to set out across the desert from Luxor to Port Sudan, meeting up with Meredith-Hardy along the way as he crossed the 400 miles (650km) of desert in the microlight.

Arriving in Port Sudan after a very enjoyable and turbulence-free desert crossing, Meredith-Hardy was embarrassed to discover that he had been reported lost in the British media and that search parties had been sent out in Egypt. The misunderstandings were resolved and the journey continued to Khartoum, where a serious engine problem with the truck resulted in a six-week wait while spares arrived from Germany.

The trip across war-torn Sudan was relatively uneventful, despite a landing on flat tyres, which had been punctured by thorns on take-off. Meredith-Hardy cleared customs at Entebbe Airport in Uganda before flying across the northern part of Lake Victoria to Kisumu in Kenya, where he was to meet up again with the support team. An engine failure just after take-off from Juba resulted in a quick return to the same strip. A radio message sent via London reached the team, who moved on from Kisumu to Nairobi to get more news. The spare engine carried on the truck was sent up at Juba by charter flight and Meredith-Hardy soon made it to Kisumu. After some rest and recuperation in Kenya, including a flight from the beach at Mombasa, the journey got under way again. After six months on the road, John Eskdale had to return to UK; he was replaced by Martyn Swain, who had been travelling around the world on his motorbike.

One of Swain's first duties in Tanzania was a three-day climb to the top of Mount Kilimanjaro, to film the microlight attempting to fly over the mountain. Equipped with oxygen, Meredith-Hardy climbed to 18,100ft but had to abandon the attempt just 1,200ft short of the summit when he ran low on fuel and oxygen. Tensions between Zambia and South Africa meant that members of the team were arrested as spies after crossing the Zambian border, but they talked their way to freedom within twenty-four hours and headed on for Zimbabwe. A trip to a local workshop immediately became necessary after another

---

Microlight Heroes: Richard Meredith-Hardy *continued*

engine failure, caused by bad fuel gumming up the spare. After some work, the microlight was shown at an International Trade Fair in Bulawayo, then flown over Victoria Falls, surely seen at their best from an open-cockpit microlight.

As they pressed on southwards, a punctured front tyre was stuffed with rags until the inner tube could be replaced, and then the pilot became ill with tick bite fever. He was given treatment, and enjoyed a brief interlude in recovery watching wildlife in the Okavango Delta and being filmed by a South African crew for a TV documentary. South Africa was finally reached via Gaberone, where white faces were received frostily after a South African bombing mission the evening before.

Over two weeks in Johannesburg, the team appeared on TV, did press interviews and photo calls and sorted out sponsorship for the last leg of the journey to Cape Town. There was another hiccup as a bureaucratic South African CAA airworthiness inspector grounded the microlight as unsafe; he was overruled by the head of the CAA, and the flight was allowed to continue. Right at the very end, the weather had the last laugh – needing only one more day's flying, Meredith-Hardy was grounded for four days by strong winds before finally reaching Cape Town.

Richard Meredith-Hardy had proved that long journeys, crossing seas, mountains and deserts, could be achieved in a flexwing microlight, and had paved the way for other adventurers.

---

2 What is a Microlight? How Does it Fly?

Microlight aircraft come in different shapes and sizes, with varying degrees of sophistication and complexity. At the simpler and least expensive end are the foot-launched microlights, while flexwing trikes take hang-glider technology to its ultimate form and three-axis microlight machines are now becoming indistinguishable from other conventional light aircraft.

What exactly is meant by the term 'microlight'? In 1999, the European Joint Aviation Authorities (JAA) agreed the definition of a microlight as follows:

A one- or two-seat aircraft having a maximum all-up weight including pilot, passenger and fuel of 450kg (990lb) for two-seat and 300kg (660lb) for single-seat

A paramotor FLM.

A powered hang-glider FLM called the Mosquito.

aircraft. The wing loading at the maximum weight authorized must not exceed 25kg per square metre or the stalling speed must not exceed 65km/h/40mph/35 knots calibrated airspeed.

In the UK, both the wing-loading and the stalling-speed criteria apply. The JAA definition permits another 10 per cent on the maximum take-off weight and 5 per cent on the stalling speed for floatplane and amphibious microlights and this is likely to be introduced into the UK as well.

Prior to the JAA definition there had been a number of different criteria across Europe, with few countries having exactly the same definition. In Britain, for example, the maximum weight limit for a two-seat microlight aircraft was 390kg (860lb), effectively ruling out many three-axis designs that were classed elsewhere as microlights or ultralights.

FOOT-LAUNCHED MICROLIGHTS

The foot-launched microlights, or FLMs, fall into two categories:

- parachute-based; a paraglider with a backpack-mounted power unit driving a propeller;
- flexwing-based; a hang-glider wing with a motor and propeller mounted on the keel tube of the wing.

Both types have to be demonstrably capable of being safely foot-launched from a horizontal surface in still air or light wind conditions – and this is a major part of their appeal. They allow flight from any convenient level area, unlike the original, unpowered hang-gliders and paragliders, which require a steep slope, a cliff with an updraft or a winch for a successful launch. In Britain, FLMs must not carry more than two persons in flight (most are, in fact, single-person machines). They must have a maximum fuel capacity of 10 litres (2.25 gallons) and a maximum unladen weight including full fuel of 60kg (130lb) for single-place and 70kg (155lb) for two-place machines.

Another appealing feature of the FLM in Britain is the fact that it is unregulated and not, therefore, subject to airworthiness requirements. It does not need a Permit to Fly, or annual inspections to revalidate the permit, both of which cost money. Neither does an FLM pilot require a licence – although only an extremely foolish individual would take to the air in an FLM without having undergone adequate training. Even those with hang-gliding, paragliding or other microlighting experience should take some training in the techniques required for the safe launching, flying and landing of an FLM.

Although FLMs are unregulated in Britain, this does not mean that they are exempt from the rules of the air and constraints that apply to pilots of other types or aircraft. FLMs must only be flown for private purposes, during the hours of daylight, and should remain in sight of the ground and clear of cloud. They are not allowed to fly at all within controlled airspace of Class A to E and may only fly in Class F and G airspace and open airspace if the visibility meets set limits. They are not allowed to fly over any congested area of a city, town or settlement or closer than 500ft to any person, vessel, building or structure, except while they are landing or taking off, or while they are hill-soaring with the engine stopped.

(To understand the different classes of airspace, refer to an aviation chart or to Brian Cosgrove's *The Microlight Pilot's Handbook*.)

The need to know the location of controlled airspace implies an ability to navigate. FLM pilots must also know that they should give way to all other types of aircraft when a conflict might occur.

Despite these restrictions, an FLM is an attractive proposition for the pilot who is happy to take to the air without wanting to cover any real distance cross country. An FLM can be bought new for around the cost of a family holiday; it can be launched from any level area; and it is extremely portable, fitting easily into a small car. The parachute type folds into a carrying bag and fits into the car's luggage space, along with the power pack, while the flexwing type will easily fit on to a roof rack.

The flexwing FLM involves a tube and fabric aerofoil Rogallo wing that pivots around the nose, with a leading-edge tube on either side, braced open by a cross-boom. The aerofoil section of the wing is achieved using leading-edge formers and a series of curved battens inserted into the wing to maintain the camber necessary to produce lift.

Powered Parachute Microlights

The powered parachute consists of a large ram-air parachute canopy attached to a wheeled trike unit on which the engine unit, ground steering controls and pilot's seat (and passenger's seat, for two-seaters) are arranged. This type of microlight is particularly weather-sensitive and has not been as successful in the UK and Europe as in the USA, although a few examples can be seen flying on still calm days.

A two-seater powered parachute, seen taking off from behind.

FLEXWING MICROLIGHTS

Flexwing microlights, also known as 'weightshifts' or 'trikes', are the ultimate development so far of the powered hang-glider. Like the flexwing FLM, they have a Rogallo tailless delta wing constructed of aluminium tubing and fabric shaped by formers and battens. The wing can be folded up and encased in a long tube-like bag for transport and storage.

The trike unit, which is connected to the wing to make the complete aircraft, consists of two main components: a base tube or hollow box section and the monopole that connects to the wing. The base tube and the monopole are held in relative position by the front (or compression) strut and form a 'chassis', on to which are bolted undercarriage members and wheels, steering apparatus, mounts for the engine and its controls, a seat assembly for the pilot (and passenger, on a two-seat version), instrument panel or binnacle, pod fairing, map boxes, braking system, fuel tanks, and all the other components that make up the modern trike.

Flexwing microlights have the engine behind the pilot and passenger seats, with a 'pusher' propeller to provide the thrust. This allows a clear and often breathtaking view of the sky ahead and the ground below. Some flexwings have almost nothing between the crew and the ground, with the crew totally exposed to the airflow, but in Europe the majority have a composite material fairing or pod to aid the aerodynamic efficiency of the aircraft and provide some protection from the elements. The open cockpit of the flexwing provides a unique flying experience; the occupants are at one with the air around them, feeling the rush of wind, aware of different smells rising from the ground below them and experiencing changes in the temperature of the air.

A modern flexwing trike, the Pegasus Quantum, with a Rotax 503 two-stroke engine.

Trikes are controlled on the ground by a pivoting nose wheel steered by foot bars on which the pilots pushes in the opposite sense of the direction of turn: pushing with the left foot to turn right, and vice versa, as with the handlebars on a bicycle. The wing is controlled in two axes by an A-frame control bar, which is pushed away from the pilot to increase the angle of attack of the wing for take-off and climb and to slow the aircraft down, and pulled towards the pilot to decrease the angle of attack to descend or to increase speed. Left turns are achieved by moving the control bar to the right, and vice versa. The A-frame control system does require a degree of physical strength,

particularly in rough or thermic air conditions, and flexwings are not always the first choice of smaller and more delicately built pilots, who often prefer three-axis controls.

Many microlight pilots prefer the flexwing or trike because of its inherent flexibility – not just in aerodynamic terms, but also in terms of simplicity and ease of operation. Most trikes can be towed behind a car on a trailer, protected by a weatherproof cover. The wing in its weatherproof bag is attached to a wing rack on the trailer and the whole craft can be kept in a garage at home, avoiding hangar fees at an airfield or microlight club strip. Keeping the aircraft at home is also convenient for maintenance,

A flexwing microlight awaits de-rigging outside the hangar.

The front strut is removed and the monopole locking device is released, allowing the wing to be lowered onto its nose with the front wheel running over the control bar. The hang bolt connecting the trike to the wing is undone and withdrawn.

The trike is wheeled away to be put on the trailer, leaving the wing to be lowered to the ground, the cross-boom tension cables released, the king post folded away and the battens withdrawn before it is folded and rolled up into the wing bag.

Ready for the road! The trike, wearing its cover and the protective propeller covers, is joined on the trailer by the wing bag. When it is firmly secured with straps and tie down cords, the aircraft can be driven away to be rigged again elsewhere, or kept in a garage until it is time to fly again.

The trike pilot's viewpoint – William Byrne's Mainair Alpha over Strangford Lough, Northern Ireland.

with easy access to tools and cleaning materials. It also avoids special trips to the airfield to work on the trike and its engine.

On arriving at the airfield or strip, a well-practised and physically strong pilot can unload a flexwing from its trailer and then rig it without help in thirty to forty-five minutes. With the aid of a knowledgeable friend, this time can be reduced to some twenty minutes. After flying, the whole machine can be de-rigged and put back on to the trailer in around the same time. The trike can also be taken on holiday, towed behind a car, van or camper, rather than flown, for flying in new areas; towing also allows a safe return home if the weather prevents further flying.

Flexwings may be flown from any suitable field or level area (such as a beach), as long as the landowner has given permission and it is clear of built-up areas. It is not necessary to find a dedicated airfield or strip with hangars. Many pilots like to operate in this way, but others prefer to pay to keep their flexwing rigged in a hangar, so that they can arrive, simply wheel the aircraft out, carry out a thorough pre-flight inspection and be in the air within a very short time. After flying, a brief post-flight inspection, and wheeling the aircraft back into the hangar, they can be on their way home. Many hangars are permanent structures that keep out the wind, rain and cold, while others are improvized shelters built for a particular aircraft. A lucky few have access to deluxe hangars with heating, air conditioning and bomb-proof doors.

A purpose-built microlight hangar.

The ultimate microlight hangar! A hardened aircraft shelter, vacated by a Tornado jet, at an operational RAF station becomes a home for the author's flexwing.

THREE-AXIS MICROLIGHTS

Three-axis microlights come in a variety of shapes and configurations. Some are virtually indistinguishable from conventional light aircraft like the Cessna 150 series, others are very distinctive in appearance. The design configurations for three-axis microlights fall into a number of categories.

Monoplanes (single-wing):

- high-wing, with the wing mounted above the fuselage;
- low-wing, with the wing mounted below the fuselage;
- mid-wing, with the wing mounted midway through the fuselage;
- canard, with a large main wing mounted at the rear of the fuselage and a smaller wing mounted forward;
- flying wing (often called Horten Formula flying wings after the German engineer who pioneered their use), where the fuselage area is incorporated into the wing surface, giving the aircraft the appearance of being just a wing, rather than a wing and fuselage.

Bi-planes (two-wing) have one upper wing and one lower wing; these are sometimes staggered, with the upper wing forward of the lower wing.

In flexwings, the two axes of control are pitch and roll; in a three-axis machine, the third axis of control is yaw.

Rans S4 and S5 microlights – examples of high-wing monoplane three-axis aircraft.

The Team MiniMax single-seater – a low-wing monoplane three-axis aircraft built from plans.

The Eurowing Goldwing canard design from around 1982; many of these are still flying today.

The Tiger Cub, a popular early biplane design dating from around 1990.

PRINCIPLES OF FLIGHT

Before looking in detail at aircraft control systems and the axes in which they work, it is first necessary to understand the basic principles of flight. Those who go on to train as pilots will inevitably study this subject in great detail.

An aircraft in flight has four main forces acting upon it: lift, drag, weight and thrust. In level flight, lift and drag are effectively the vertical and horizontal components of the total force of the air acting on the aircraft moving through it. This force is called the total reaction (*see* the diagram on page 35). For an aircraft to be in level flight, lift must be equal to and opposite to the weight.

Lift

Wings generate lift. That lift is partially produced by direct reaction and partially by the creation of a pressure differential about the wing.

Do you remember as a child holding your hand out of the window of a moving car, and feeling a force trying to pull it back away from the direction in which the car was moving? The *total reaction* experienced by the hand was acting only horizontally and was therefore all *drag*. If the forward part of your hand is raised slightly, an upward force is produced. The total reaction is now acting in a slightly upward direction. Although the *drag* is still acting horizontally, there is now also an element of *lift*, acting vertically. This *lift* has been produced by the hand giving the air a downwards deflection, or *downwash*.

The other part of lift is *pressure differential*. Daniel Bernoulli, a Swiss professor of mathematics, discovered that in the stream-

34

Lift, drag, weight, thrust.

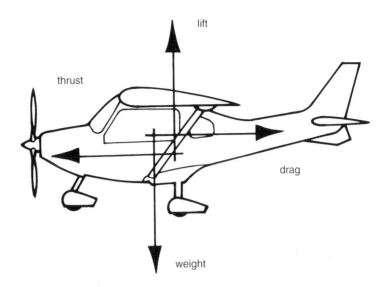

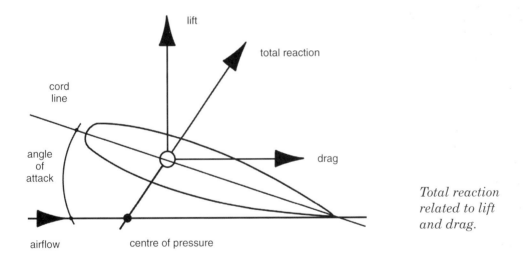

Total reaction related to lift and drag.

line flow of an ideal fluid the sum of the energies is constant. This is known as Bernoulli's Theorem. In low-speed aerodynamics, very much applicable to microlights, it is easiest to assume that air acts like an ideal fluid, simplifying the theory by disregarding those factors such as compressibility, changes of heat energy and potential energy, which are important in high-speed aerodynamics.

To understand what happens around a wing aerofoil section, look at the flow of air through a Venturi, or a convergent/divergent duct. The 'streamlines' drawn through the Venturi represent the possible paths of a particle of air. If smoke were allowed to flow through the Venturi with the air, as in wind-tunnel tests, the way the streamlines accelerate and then decelerate as they pass through would be easy to see. For a steady

Downwash of airflow producing lift.

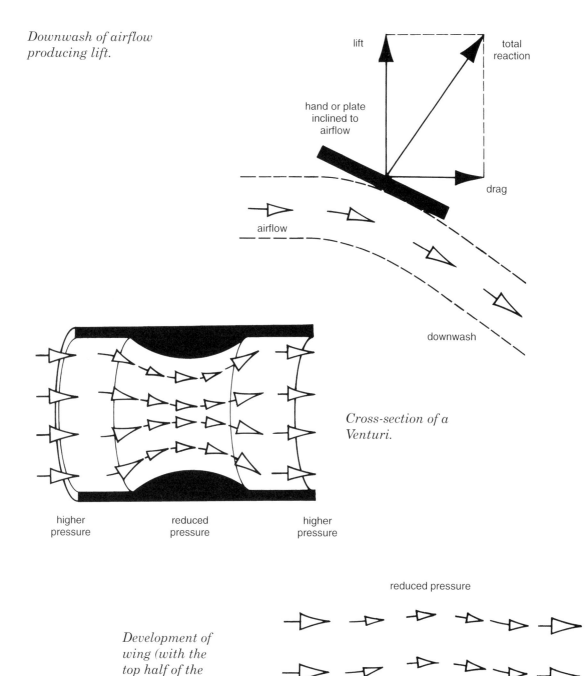

lift

total reaction

hand or plate inclined to airflow

drag

airflow

downwash

Cross-section of a Venturi.

higher pressure

reduced pressure

higher pressure

reduced pressure

Development of wing (with the top half of the Venturi removed).

streamlined flow there must be a constant mass flow through the Venturi and, consequently, the air must speed up through the narrow part of the Venturi. This, in accordance with Bernoulli's Theorem, causes a proportional reduction of pressure in the narrow part; put simply:

$$\frac{\text{kinetic}}{\text{energy}} + \frac{\text{pressure}}{\text{energy}} = \text{constant}$$

With the top half of the Venturi off, the bottom half retains similar flow characteristics. The airflow pattern is similar to that which occurs over the upper surface of a cambered airfoil section when set at a zero-degree angle of attack. If a symmetrical wing section meets the airflow at a zero-degree angle of attack, the air speeds up over both upper and lower surfaces equally, and there is an equal pressure drop over both surfaces, and no lift is produced.

When a symmetrical wing section meets the airflow at a small positive angle of attack, say, plus 4 degrees, the air flowing over the upper surface speeds up by a convergence of the streamlines and produces a reduction in pressure. (In reality, most aircraft wings are not entirely symmetrical but in order to grasp the concept, it is easier to assume that they are.) The air flowing below the wing also speeds up a little but produces a smaller reduction in pressure because the streamlines converge to a lesser degree.

The difference between these two reductions in pressure is *pressure differential lift*.

Drag

In flight, all surfaces of an aircraft produce an aerodynamic force. *Total drag* is the sum of all the different components of this force, which act parallel and opposite to the direction of flight and, in straight and level unaccelerated flight, have to be balanced by *thrust*. For maximum efficiency, the drag experienced by an aircraft as it passes through the air should be as little as possible. The higher the drag, the more thrust is required, and the steeper the glide if the engine should stop.

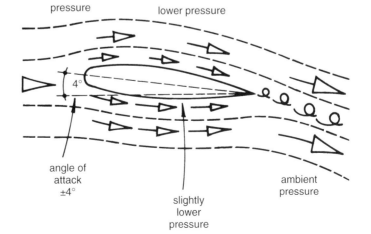

Pressure distribution around a symmetrical airfoil section at a small angle of attack.

ambient pressure

lower pressure

4°

angle of attack ±4°

slightly lower pressure

ambient pressure

There are four components of drag: three types of *zero lift drag*, and *lift-dependent drag*.

Zero Lift Drag

When an aircraft is flying at a zero lift angle of attack, the resultant of all the aerodynamic forces acts parallel and opposite to the direction of flight and is known as *zero lift drag*. Its three components are *surface friction drag*, *form drag* and *interference drag*.

Viscosity is the tendency of a fluid to adhere to the surface over which it is flowing. The viscosity of air causes a thin layer to be dragged along with a moving aircraft. This is known as the *boundary layer* and generally varies in thickness from about 0.07 to 0.7 of an inch (1.5 to 15mm). The amount of *surface friction drag* produced is determined by the nature and thickness of the boundary layer.

In theory, *surface friction drag* can be minimized by maintaining a smooth 'laminar flow' surface over as much of the wing as possible. In practice, even a few dead insects or some raindrops on the wing will make this flow turbulent. Very few microlights, except the latest composite three-axis designs, can have a truly smooth wing surface; flexwings are usually covered in a fabric sail, while non-composite three-axis designs feature a taught fabric covering. Even with a smooth, composite wing, the smallest scratch or imperfection will produce turbulence that will increase surface friction drag.

Microlight designers are constantly striving to keep the boundary layer as thin as possible by using smooth surfaces, flush rivets and large smooth panels, particularly on the leading edge (front part of the wing), where this is most critical.

Form drag is caused by turbulent wake – effectively, the result of air resisting an object trying to pass through it and forcing

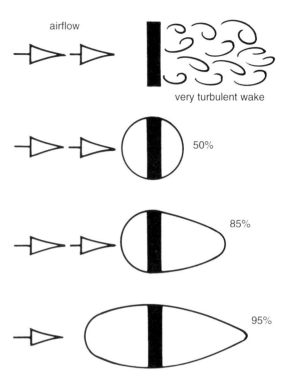

The effect of streamlining on form drag.

the air to separate around it. One example is the blast of air felt at the side of a busy road each time a car or truck passes; this is the turbulent wake caused by the vehicle making a 'hole' in the air through which it is passing. Changing the shape of an aircraft may reduce form drag. Streamlining and keeping the frontal areas as small as possible are the main methods of minimizing the form drag of bodies and wing sections. Fitting a streamlined composite pod to a flexwing microlight trike will not only provide the pilot and passenger with some protection from the elements, but will also reduce form drag.

On any aircraft, the total drag is greater than the sum of the values of drag for each separate part. Interference drag is the additional drag that results from airflow interference at the wing/fuselage junction, and other such junctions. It can be reduced by the use of fillets or fairings at these junctions, but not eliminated completely.

Lift-Dependent (or Induced) Drag

To stay in the air an aircraft must produce lift. Unfortunately, the means by which this lift is produced creates extra drag. This extra drag is known as *lift-dependent drag* and is very apparent at high angles of attack. When an aircraft is flying and its wing is producing positive lift, the pressure differences between the upper and lower surfaces of the wing cause air to spill around the wing tips from the lower surface to the top surface

The result of this spillage is the formation of a vortex at the wing tip. When a large airliner lands, smoke from the tyres drifts up into the wing-tip vortex and flows in a spiral as it passes through it, giving a good impression of how the air is moving around the edge of the wing.

Another result of the pressure differential

is that the angle of airflow rearwards of the wing is not the same over the wing as under it. Mixing of airflow occurs where the flows meet all along the trailing edge of the wing and a sheet of vortices is formed. Under conditions of high lift production, such as manoeuvres, the pressure difference between upper and lower wing surfaces will be greatly increased, resulting in stronger wing-tip and trailing-edge vortices. The production of these vortices absorbs energy from the airflow and the value of total drag increases as vortex production increases. This increase is known as induced or vortex drag and is the main component of lift-dependant drag.

The faster a wing is moving through the air, the smaller the tip and the trailing-edge vortices, because the airflow is being affected by the pressure differential for a shorter time.

The *aspect ratio* of the wing is also a factor. The longer and thinner the wing, the higher the aspect ratio and the smaller the tip lift losses due to vortex generation.

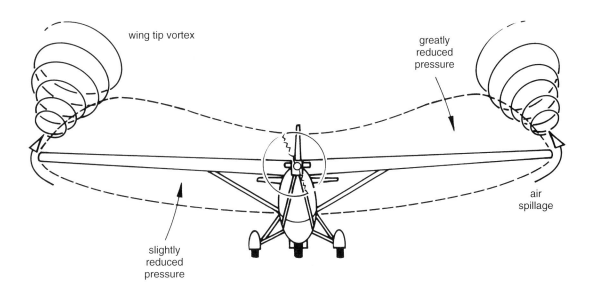

Spillage of air around a wing in flight.

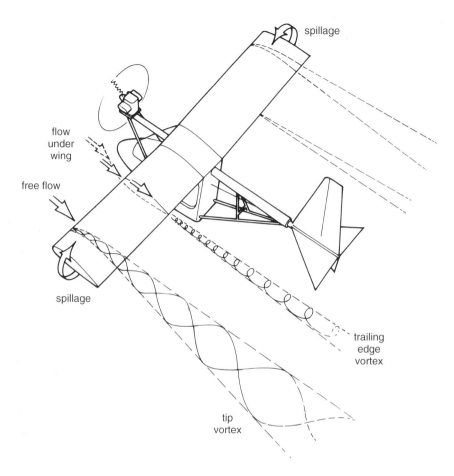

Formation of wing-tip and trailing-edge vortices.

This is why gliders have such long thin wings; they may be less structurally efficient but aerodynamically they are much more suitable.

Total Drag and Thrust
The total drag of an aircraft is equal to the sum of the zero lift drag and the lift-dependant drag of all its parts. Flexwing microlight designs are essentially slow and 'draggy', although modern fabric technology has allowed greater tension of wing surfaces, making the latest flex-wings stiffer, faster and more efficient. Three-axis machines, particularly the smooth sleek composite designs, rather than the older tube and fabric types, are much more aerodynamically efficient and less 'draggy'. The more drag an aircraft has, the more thrust it requires to maintain level flight. For this reason, three-axis microlight designs usually offer a much better performance in terms of speed and fuel consumption for a given engine size and power output than flexwings.

Stalling
Microlights are limited in weight by their very definition! For an aircraft of a given weight, an equal amount of lift must be

produced for the aircraft to fly. More lift is required if the aircraft is to climb; less lift than weight will cause it to descend. There is a particular point at which lift will suddenly reduce and level or climbing flight will turn rapidly into a descent if action is not taken quickly. This point is known as the *stall*.

An aircraft that has stalled is out of control and remains so until correct recovery action is taken. Losing control of an aircraft by stalling close to the ground, particularly during take-off or when landing, is a very serious event. If there is insufficient height for the pilot to take correct recovery action, a crash will be the inevitable result. It is essential, therefore, to know what a stall is, how to recognize the symptoms leading to it and how to recover from it.

Increasing the angle of attack of an aerofoil or wing section increases the lift produced. There comes a point, however, at which the angle of attack becomes too steep to allow a smooth enough airflow over the upper wing surfaces for the maintenance of the pressure differential between the upper and lower wing surface (which produces lift). This angle of attack is known as the critical or stalling angle. In subsonic flight, for a given aerofoil shape, the stall will usually occur at about the same critical angle, normally between 15 and 17 degrees. In a stall, the relatively smooth (although still somewhat turbulent) boundary layer over the upper surface of the wing breaks up and creates a larger area of turbulence behind it (*see* the diagram). This turbulence can often be felt through the controls and the airframe as a 'buffet'.

The basic stalling speed of an aircraft is that speed below which an aircraft of a given weight, with the engine throttled back, can no longer maintain level flight or at which the pilot no longer has full control. It follows that, if there is any

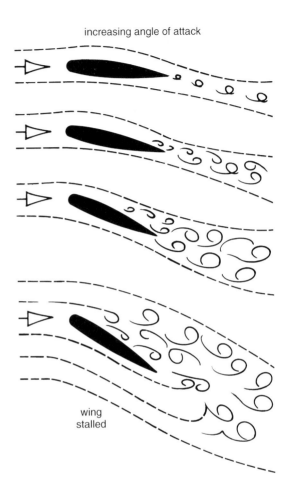

increasing angle of attack

wing stalled

A stalled aerofoil.

increase in weight, the provision of the extra lift necessary for level flight at the stall must come from higher speed. More weight will therefore increase the stalling speed. When an aircraft is being manoeuvred, such as during a steep turn, additional lift is required. This lift requirement imposes an equal amount of apparent weight, essentially the same as extra weight, on the aircraft. The effect is the same as adding additional weight to the aircraft – the speed at which the aircraft stalls increases.

If you close the throttle on a microlight, and use the controls to try to maintain level flight, the following sequence of symptoms will occur:

1. Before the stall: airspeed will decrease; controls become 'sloppy'; the nose rises; buffet gradually builds up.
2. At the stall: the aircraft descends; there is heavy buffet; the nose and possibly a wing will drop as one wing stalls before the other.

Microlight aircraft generally have a low stalling speed and, usually, benign stalling characteristics. This means that they do not stall viciously, with fast nose and wing drop, requiring dramatic and rapid recovery action. Indeed, many microlights simply 'mush along' at the stall, losing height but not nosing down steeply or dropping a wing.

Flaps

Flaps are movable surfaces that extend down from underneath the wings of three-axis aircraft. They are fitted to some three-axis microlights and are usually operated by a lever in the cockpit or near to the pilot's seat. Recent innovations in hang-glider design allow a form of flap to be fitted to flexwings too, and the design may soon be seen on flexwing microlights.

Flaps can enhance the lift provided by the wing and allow the aircraft to fly more slowly without stalling by effectively increasing the camber of the wing and, thus, the lift it provides. They are most often used when approaching to land and landing, to provide a steeper approach with a more nose-down attitude, allowing a better view of the runway and a slower approach speed. They can also be used to provide extra lift on take-off. As flaps produce more drag, they are set to the 'up' position when in normal flight.

The type most commonly used on microlights is the plain flap, although several microlight designs use flaperons, a combination aileron and flap. Flaps cannot be used on canard designs.

CONTROLS

Having understood the basic principles of aerodynamics, how does the pilot control an aircraft in flight? There are three axes of control: *pitch*, *roll* and *yaw*.

Pitch is the position of the aircraft's nose and tail relative to the horizon; 'pitch up' means the nose is above the horizon and the tail is down; 'pitch down' is vice versa. Changes in pitch affect the angle of attack of the wing, which is related to lift.

Roll is the position of the aircraft's wings relative to the horizon; in a roll to the right, the right wing goes down and the left wing moves up, and vice versa.

Yaw is the rotation of the aircraft around an axis passing vertically through its centre or gravity. Imagine sitting on an office chair on castors; if you push with your feet in either direction, the chair will twist in the opposite direction. This is equivalent to the yawing motion in an aircraft.

Flexwing controls operate in the two axes of pitch and roll, while three-axis machines are controlled in all three axes.

Three-Axis Controls

These controls most commonly consist of *ailerons*, *elevators* and *rudder*. There are other forms of controls, using spoilers, flaperons, rudder with no ailerons, all-moving tails and tailplanes, but the following descriptions cover the basics. There are many different ways for the pilot to operate these controls, but the most conventional is the stick (sometimes called 'joystick') and rudder pedals. (In this very basic explanation of three-axis controls and their effects,

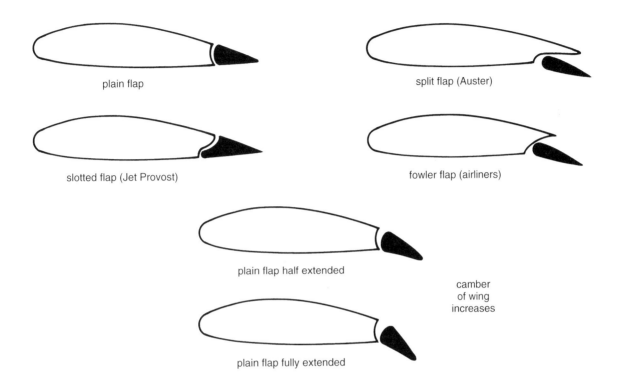

Some examples of aircraft flaps.

the stick and rudder system will be used to describe how the controls are operated by the pilot.)

Ailerons
Ailerons are movable surfaces set into the trailing edge of each wing. They work in opposite senses to each other: when the left aileron rises, the right aileron lowers, and vice versa, and the aircraft moves in the rolling plane. This movement is known as *banking*. As the aircraft banks in one direction, the secondary effect of banking, involving a sideslip towards the lower wing, is for the aircraft to turn in that direction. To initiate a turn, the pilot banks the aircraft in the direction of the turn. The ailerons are operated by moving the control stick from side to side.

Ailerons are also used to counteract the effect of crosswinds on take-off and especially on landing, by keeping the into-wind wing down and preventing the aircraft drifting off line in a downwind direction. When coming in to land with a crosswind from the right, the pilot needs to apply a little right aileron control to keep the right wing slightly down. This will prevent the aircraft from drifting to the left off the runway or landing strip centre line. This sort of 'wing-down' landing results in the aircraft landing initially on one wheel and

43

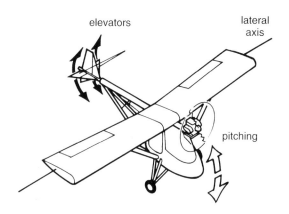

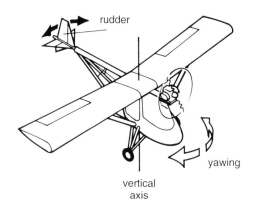

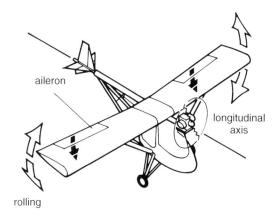

The three axes of control and the controls that effect them.

requires skill and practice.

A turn using just the ailerons will result in a yaw towards the outside of the turn and a less efficient passage through the air. To counteract this adverse yaw, the rudder is used to produce a balanced turn.

Rudder

The rudder is a movable surface set into or attached to the fin, the vertical surface of the tailplane at the rear of a conventional three-axis aircraft. The rudder works in the same way as a rudder on a boat.

The rudder is operated with two linked foot pedals; if the left foot is pushed forward, left rudder is applied and the right pedal moves backwards, and vice versa. As the rudder is applied, one side deflects into the airflow and pushes the tail of the aircraft in the opposite direction in the yawing plane. Applying left rudder causes the aircraft to yaw to the left.

It is possible to use the rudder alone to bank and turn the aircraft but this results in a slip towards the outside of the turn, so use of the rudder is co-ordinated with use of the ailerons in order to produce a balanced turn.

Elevators

The elevators are movable surfaces set into the horizontal part of the tailplane at the rear of the aircraft on either side of the fin. They work together in the same sense and control the aircraft in the pitching plane.

The elevators are operated by moving the aircraft control stick forwards and backwards. If the control stick is moved backwards, both elevators are deflected upwards into the airflow. They push the tail of the aircraft down and cause the nose to rise, slowing the aeroplane unless power is increased. If sufficient power is available the aircraft will then climb. If the control stick is moved forwards, the elevators are deflected downwards, pushing the tail up and causing the nose to point downwards. The aircraft will then descend and accelerate.

Three-axis aircraft are manoeuvred by using a combination of all three controls to move them in all three planes of movement. Power is also used with the controls to climb the aircraft and control the rate of descent. The co-ordinated use of controls together with power is the secret of efficient flying and its perfection requires careful training and practice. Student microlight pilots study the effects of controls and power in extensive detail, learning to control their aircraft safely and to fly it within its safe performance 'envelope'. Cosgrove's highly recommended *The Microlight Pilot's Handbook* is a major work of reference for British microlight pilots studying for their licence.

Flexwing Controls

In the trike configuration, the flexwing pilot sits in a tricycle unit, to which the engine is attached; the whole trike unit is suspended underneath the wing via a monopole attached to the wing's hangpoint. In the FLM configuration, the engine is either mounted on to the wing's main keel tube, and the pilot suspended underneath in a harness; alternatively, the engine and the pilot are underneath the wing in a harness, both attached to the wing's hangpoint.

All these configurations have the same control system, known as weightshift – the pilot literally shifts the weight of his or her body, or that of the trike, relative to the wing. This is done by exerting a force on the A-frame control bar that is rigidly attached to the wing. Before take-off, when the trike or pilot is fixed in place by contact with the ground, moving the control bar moves the wing up or down or from side to side. In the air, the weight being shifted acts as a pendulum upon the wing and causes its centre of gravity to move. When

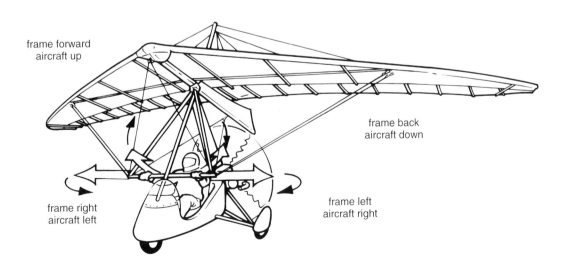

Weightshift controls.

this happens, the wing will move in the direction in which the weight has shifted. In simple terms:

To turn right: push the control bar to the left, shifting the weight to the right and the wing will roll to the right and initiate a turn to the right.

To turn left: push the control bar to the right, shifting the weight to the left and the wing will roll to the left and initiate a turn to the left.

To increase speed: pull the control bar towards you; the angle of attack will decrease and the aircraft will speed up.

To decrease speed: push the control bar away from you; the angle of attack will increase and the aircraft will slow down.

To climb: increase power and adjust the control bar position to increase height at the desired rate and airspeed.

To descend: decrease power and adjust the control bar to reduce height at the desired rate and airspeed.

In order to climb, there must be enough power available; trying to climb too steeply, even with full power, will cause the aircraft to stall. When descending, the engine is usually throttled back; otherwise, the aircraft will speed up, possibly to a speed that is not safe for the aircraft's design characteristics. Keeping within the aircraft's speed and handling capabilities – 'flying within the envelope' – is an important part of the pilot's skills.

Why do weightshift controls not deal with the third axis of yaw? Flexwings cannot be yawed in the same way as three-axis machines, but their design characteristics and shape do control the adverse yaw in a turn. As the wing turns there is greater form drag on the rear of the side of the wing into the turn and this causes the whole wing to 'weathercock' into the direction of the turn.

Control System Differences

The differences between three-axis and flexwing controls are exactly opposite to each other – careful conversion training should be undertaken by pilots moving from one control system to another. To bank and turn a three-axis machine, the pilot moves the control stick in the direction of the turn; the flexwing pilot moves the control frame in the opposite direction. The flexwing pilot pushes the control bar forwards/away to raise the nose of the aircraft while the three-axis pilot pulls the stick backwards in order to achieve the same effect. Many an experienced three-axis pilot has been caught out by this difference in the most critical phase of flight, the landing, when flying a flexwing microlight for the first time.

While in the air, the flexwing pilot has no use for the steering bar that steers the aircraft on the ground; the three-axis pilot uses the rudder pedals to co-ordinate turns in the air and to steer the aircraft on the ground. Again, these controls on a flexwing work in the opposite sense to those on a three-axis machine. To turn left on the ground, the flexwing pilot pushes forward with the right foot on the steering bar while the three-axis pilot pushes forward on the left rudder pedal. This difference on the ground must be remembered when taxiing, taking off and landing.

FLM Controls

The flexwing FLM's controls work in exactly the same way as those on the flexwing trike, although directional control on the ground depends entirely on the pilot, who runs along the ground both to take off and to come to a stop after landing.

Paramotor (parachute-type) FLM controls, and the controls for powered parachutes, work in the same way as the modern parachute canopy – the trailing edge of one side of the canopy is pulled down by the pilot

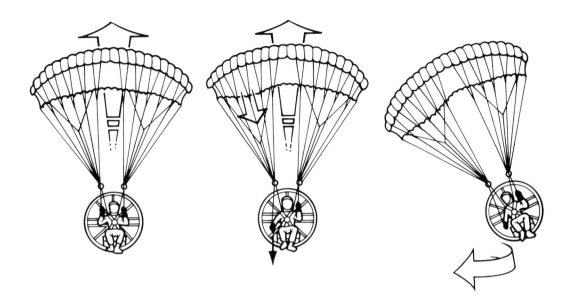

Parachute FLM controls.

tugging on a toggle attached to the harness. As the trailing edge depresses, drag on that side of the canopy is increased and it slows down, while the other side of the canopy keeps flying at the same speed. The result is that the whole parachute turns in the direction of the drag. In other words, the pilot pulls down on the right toggle to turn right, and on the left toggle to turn left. Pulling down on both toggles brakes or slows the canopy and this method is used when landing. Experienced FLM pilots learn to stop the parachute just above the ground and then just 'step down' to an impressive landing, without having to run at all.

The engine is accelerated to make the parachute FLM climb and the power is reduced or turned off to descend.

Microlight Heroines: Eve Jackson

In April 1986, Eve Jackson, just 26 years old, left Britain in 'Gertie' – a tiny CFM (Cook's Flying Machines) Shadow three-axis microlight – to start the longest-ever microlight flight of the time. Her plan was to fly, without any back-up crew, from London to Australia. Many in the aviation world felt that, without ground support, the odds would be stacked against her; some doubted that she would ever make it.

Eve Jackson was not a hugely experienced microlight pilot with thousands of flying hours and many cross-country flights behind her. In fact, although she had qualified as a pilot, she had only around 100 hours in her logbook. She had found it very difficult to attract major sponsors for her flight and had to rely on a number of smaller supporters, and her own resources. Sensibly, she elected not to fly in weather that was too extreme for her experience, choosing to complete the journey safely, however long it took.

Microlight Heroines: Eve Jackson *continued*

The Shadow had extra fuel tanks fitted to extend its range to 500 miles (800km), to allow it to negotiate the sea crossings. The route was planned via France, Germany, what was then Czechoslovakia and Yugoslavia, Greece, Turkey, Syria, Jordan, Saudi Arabia, the United Arab Emirates, Oman, Pakistan, India, Bangladesh, Burma, Thailand, Malaysia, Indonesia, Papua New Guinea, before finally reaching Australia.

Inevitably, there were bureaucratic delays along the way; in many countries, it was not usual to see a woman flying a small aeroplane solo across the world. Navigation over the featureless deserts of Saudi Arabia was one of the biggest worries – this was before Global Positioning Systems had became widely available; the problem was safely overcome by following oil pipelines.

By mid-October 1986, pilot and microlight reached the Indian sub-continent, passing the half-way point of the total journey of 12,500 miles (20,000km) just before reaching Delhi.

Here, Eve Jackson ran into her first major problem. Gertie's Permit to Fly was soon to expire and a valid permit was vital in getting permission from the Thai authorities to overfly their country. David Cook, the brilliant designer of the Shadow series of aircraft and a director of CFM, had to travel out to India to carry out the necessary inspection and check flight, sending the paperwork back to UK by telex so that a new certificate of validity could be issued. It was the first time that a permit revalidation for a UK-registered microlight had been done in this way, but the Civil Aviation Authority readily accepted this solution. While the pilot waited in Delhi, Gertie's Rotax 447 engine was returned to the UK to be stripped down, inspected, serviced and reassembled.

Shortly after the engine was returned to India and reinstalled in Gertie, it seized up on a local pleasure flight, making a forced landing necessary. Happily, no damage was done. After getting the engine sorted out, the two were soon on their way again and, after some slight engine problems in Rangoon, by mid-February they were leaving Kuala Lumpur in Malaysia. Following further bureaucratic delays in Indonesia, they were soon island-hopping on the final leg of the journey towards the coast of Australia.

Arriving in Darwin, in the Northern Territory, Eve Jackson took her place in the history of aviation, setting a new record for the longest microlight flight, and becoming the first person ever to fly from London to Australia in a microlight. Having left home as a relatively inexperienced and unknown pilot, she had arrived in Sydney fifteen months later to international acclaim. She had shown a remarkable determination, undertaking an epic journey without any support crew on the ground. Her achievements also helped establish the reputation of the CFM Shadow aircraft, which won a British Design Award during her flight.

Enjoying the view on a crisp English morning, an early Mainair Rapier.

Richard Meredith-Hardy in a Pegasus AX2000 over Italy.

Having fun in a French Fun GT503.

The delightful CFM Shadow flown by Paul Dewhurst.

The Snowbird: old but lovely to fly.

BELOW: *A twin-engined microlight,
the unusual three-axis Lazair.*

Gently does it: a paramotor FLM.

The Cyclone AX3, a popular three-axis design.

Channel crossing: two Pegasus flexwings between England and France.

Number two to land: arriving by air at the annual microlight trade fair at Popham Airfield in Hampshire, England.

Clear on top: keeping clear of cloud and in sight of the surface in a Mainair Blade 912.

A Thruster over the English countryside.

French-manufactured Air Creation Clipper, this one registered in Germany

Heading for home: the Mainair Blade 912 of first solo round-the-world microlight pilot Colin Bodill, seen over icebergs off the coast of Greenland.

Follow me! Colin Bodill leads solo helicopter pilot Jennifer Murray over cloud above the sea on their epic round-the-world journey.

BELOW: *Open-air fun in a British-registered, French-built Fun GT.*

ABOVE: *The evergreen Pegasus XL about to make a textbook touchdown.*

Brian Milton takes time out to see a baseball stadium in the USA during his global circumnavigation in a Pegasus Quantum 912.

BELOW: *The Doodlebug, a powered hang-glider FLM, being flown by Ben Ashman.*

Marie Jeffrey's superb shot of Colin Bodill's Mainair Blade approaching Sydney harbour bridge.

An old favourite, the Medway Hybred Raven.

RIGHT: *Brian Milton and Keith Reynolds flying over a mountain pass in the GT Global Pegasus Quantum 912.*

Colin Bodill over the Sydney Opera House in his Mainair Blade 912 after his flight to Australia.

The unusual but popular Mistral, a closed-cockpit biplane microlight from Belgium.

Winter wonderland! A Spectrum Beaver fitted with Full Lotus floats by a frozen waterfall.

The beautiful Murphy Renegade II biplane; this one is from Germany.

3 Learning to Fly a Microlight

HOW IT USED TO BE DONE

In the early days of microlights, many pilots taught themselves to fly by trial and error. Sadly, relying only on instinct and luck, a number of aspiring pilots were killed and many others injured. Others showed better judgement in doing research into the principles of flight and how aircraft controls worked before actually taking to the air. Some of the more persistent became exceptionally able microlight pilots and went on to become flying instructors, bringing new generations of pilots and instructors into microlighting.

In the early days, single-seat microlight training involved instructors shouting instructions from the ground as the student struggled into the air. Increased use of radio allowed the student to climb higher while listening to hear the instructor's directions. Today, microlight instruction is given on two-seat aircraft, with the instructor able to take the controls whenever necessary.

WHO CAN LEARN TO FLY?

Persistence and a good deal of natural ability are still the best qualities for learning to fly a microlight quickly. The instinctive pilot comes from any walk of life. The majority of pilots are not 'naturals', however, and will have to work hard to achieve a high degree of competence, without ever becoming brilliant. Flying is a constant learning process and even the most gifted and experienced pilots are constantly learning throughout their flying career.

The first step on the path towards becoming a pilot is to be absolutely sure that you want to do it. Flying training requires real commitment from the student pilot and from the instructor. The instructor will soon sense if the student does not have the necessary desire to succeed and will probably advise against wasting any more money. Most beginners are very keen but there is a high fall-out rate in flying training.

If you think that you would like to learn to fly, have a trial lesson or get a microlight pilot to take you flying, to help you make your mind up. You will either find it exhilarating or terrifying. Everyone is different. Some people have a very high fear threshold and remain calm in the face of a potentially dangerous situation, while others can be paralysed with fear. The brave person is the one who suffers fear and overcomes it, rather than the one who feels no fear in the first place. For the student pilot, a feeling of fear or apprehension concentrates the mind on learning the correct lessons and staying safe. Successful flying is about risk management. Skilled pilots assess the risk, know their own capabilities and the capabilities of their aircraft, and can manage the risk involved in flying to stay within safe boundaries.

Today's pilot is no longer the square-jawed and hairy-chested hero of the old images. Modern control systems have

This elegantly attired aviator evokes the dash and daring of a bygone era,
when England's enemies trembled!

removed many of the physical demands of flying, and a significant number of women are now involved in airsports. (Some types of microlight flying do still involve a degree of physical challenge; *see* Medical and Physical Requirements, below.)

Learning to drive a car on today's busy roads is an accumulation of skills, knowledge and the ability to make the right judgements and decisions. Learning to fly is essentially the same process, but requires an appreciation of a higher number of factors. Anyone who has been able to learn to drive a car is likely to be able to learn to fly a microlight, but it will probably take a little longer.

MEDICAL AND PHYSICAL REQUIREMENTS

Different countries have different medical requirements for microlight pilots. In Britain, a simple system of self-declaration of medical fitness has been in use for some years. The pilot signs a certificate to state that he or she does not suffer from any of a number of particular medical conditions which would potentially be hazardous for flying. This certificate is counter-signed by the pilot's doctor; in this way, someone who is clearly not fit to fly, because of a known medical condition, is prevented from doing so. The system may be relaxed further, so that pilots who only wish to fly solo may not require a counter-signature on their medical certificate.

Some other countries require no medical certificate at all while others require a full medical examination to determine fitness to fly. Generally speaking, anyone who is fit enough to drive a car is fit enough to fly a microlight. Reasonably good eyesight is required, to be able to read instruments in the aircraft and to keep a good look-out for other aircraft, but those who wear spectacles or contact lenses to correct their vision to a reasonable standard can also fly. The normal range of movement of arms and legs is usually required, in order to operate the aircraft's controls. However, many disabled pilots fly microlights with control systems that have been adapted for them. Reasonably good hearing is useful when listening to the radio, but many pilots still fly without a radio in their aircraft.

A prohibitive condition is one that could suddenly lead to incapacitation in the air. People who suffer from epilepsy, fits, recurrent fainting, giddiness or blackouts, heart disease, high blood pressure that cannot be controlled by drugs, insulin-controlled diabetes, any psychiatric condition or any other disorder liable to cause sudden incapacitation are likely to be prevented from flying.

At some stage, all pilots have to accept that age will prevent them from flying. However, many microlight pilots in their seventies still undertake long and challenging flights; the age itself should not be a barrier, providing good health is enjoyed.

A number of physical considerations need to be taken into account. Foot-launched microlights require a good standard of physical fitness, strength, and often agility. In hot weather, the take-off run needs to be longer and faster than in colder weather, when the air is denser and provides more lift and thrust from a propeller. Only a fit, strong pilot can cope with this. Flexwing microlights require a degree of strength to move the control bar, particularly in roll and when the air is turbulent or thermic and suddenly lifts one side of the wing. Flexwings and FLMs are open-cockpit and open-air aircraft respectively and provide less protection from the elements than three-axis microlights. If you are not particularly fit or strong, and like to keep warm in the winter, choose a three-axis microlight with a closed cockpit.

TRAINING

If you really want to learn to fly microlights, and are medically and physically capable of doing so, you now need to consider training. Training comes in two parts, flying training and ground school.

Flying training

Flying training introduces the student to the microlight and teaches safe handling through all the stages of flight. Training is usually broken down into a number of exercises that are demonstrated and explained by the instructor, and then imitated and practised by the student, until a satisfactory standard of proficiency is achieved and maintained.

Before flying, the safety inspection of the aircraft must be carried out, and the aircraft, pilot and instructor must be prepared for flying. The aircraft must be confirmed as being in a thoroughly airworthy condition, properly assembled or rigged, with sufficient fuel for the flight and some in reserve. The engine must be working properly and all moving parts, particularly control systems and vital instruments, must be checked and found to be working correctly. Student pilot and instructor must be correctly dressed, and well fed and watered. It's well worth visiting the toilet too, to avoid discomfort or embarrassment in the air, particularly in cold weather!

The Mistral, a splendid Belgian biplane microlight, and a good example of a closed-cockpit three-axis microlight. About fourteen of these unusual machines fly in the UK, and there are many more across Europe.

Once the engine has been started safely and warmed up, the aircraft must be taxied correctly to the take-off point, giving way to other aircraft as necessary, and the pre-take-off checks carried out. When it is all clear and safe to take off, the aircraft must be accelerated into the wind and a controlled take-off and climb-out performed.

While in the air, the student pilot must learn to do the following safely:

- climb;
- descend;
- turn;
- anticipate and recover from a stall;
- navigate;
- communicate (when radio is carried); and

- constantly monitor the performance of the aircraft and the fuel burn.

The student must know what to do in a range of emergency situations and should practise forced landings until the instructor is sure that, in the event of an engine failure, the student will be able to land the microlight safely in a suitable field or other flat area, such as a beach.

On returning to base, or arriving at another airfield or strip, the student pilot must learn to join the circuit safely and then make a safe approach and landing before taxiing to an appropriate parking area. There, the engine is stopped, the aircraft vacated and checks are made to ensure that

The superb CFM Shadow about to touch down on a beach.

it is safely parked and, if necessary, tied down. If the aircraft is to be de-rigged after flight, the student should also learn the correct procedure for doing this and, if appropriate, for loading the aircraft on to a trailer.

Once the student has demonstrated competence to the entire satisfaction of the instructor, the biggest milestone in any pilot's flying career is reached – the first solo. The student pilot takes off for the first time alone, usually rather apprehensively, to fly some circuits. All pilots remember their first solo for the rest of their lives; the sense of achievement and elation when the aircraft is safely back on the ground makes it a great occasion. There are many different ways of a marking a first solo, from a celebratory drink or party (usually at the student's expense), to a commemora-

tive photograph of the student and the aircraft.

After the first solo, more advanced flying exercises are flown. These include solo cross-country navigation tasks, with landings at other airfields or strips, and consolidation training, both with the instructor and solo. The final flying training hurdle before the granting of a licence is the GFT (General Flying Test), which demonstrates to an examiner that the student pilot is sufficiently competent in all aspects of handling the aircraft, and in the airmanship required to safely fly a microlight around the circuit or from place to place. Once the GFT has been passed, and all the ground school exams have been successfully completed, the student pilot can apply for a microlight pilot's licence.

Ground School

In addition to flying training, the student pilots must also learn a number of ground-school subjects that are considered vital to the development of a safe and competent pilot. This can be achieved by doing one or more of the following:

- attending ground-school lessons given by your flying instructor or another qualified instructor;
- study of books such as Cosgrove's *The Microlight Pilot's Handbook*;
- studying on a computer using one of the many interactive learning packages now available on CD-ROM.

The best results are always achieved by a combination of attending lessons and private study. Those who are not particularly confident in their academic ability should not be put off by the thought of having to go back to the classroom and take written exams. All the ground-school subjects relate to what goes on in the air while flying and the facts are much easier to understand when put into context.

The subjects usually taught in ground school and confirmed by written examinations are as follows:

- general or technical, including principles of flight, engines and airframes, ancillary equipment;
- meteorology;
- navigation;
- air law; and
- human performance and limitations.

The general or technical subject ensures that the student pilot understands how the aircraft flies, and how its engine and control systems work. It also covers aircraft performance and the many different factors that can affect it both in the air and when taking off and landing.

Meteorology lessons give a sufficient understanding of the weather, and how it affects the performance and safety of the aircraft, for the pilot to know when it is safe to fly and when it is not. This includes being able to anticipate and plan for changes to the weather during a flight, especially if it is a long cross-country flight, or a touring flight.

Navigation training on the ground provides the pilot with the necessary skills and knowledge to plan before a flight and then fly to that plan, knowing at all times the aircraft's location and how to get where he or she wants to go. The more navigation is included in flight planning on the ground, the easier it is to navigate once in the air.

Air law training ensures that the pilot understands how the law applies to each individual, including when and where microlights may fly, what documents must be held in the pilots possession, what rules must be obeyed and how to ensure that both pilot and aircraft are capable and safe for the flights planned.

'Human performance and limitations' is a relatively new subject in aviation and covers all the different factors that can affect the way a pilot performs in flight. These range from the effects of tiredness, alcohol, drugs, lack of oxygen and cold to misperceptions and misjudgements caused by stress, anxiety, complacency or confusion. The knowledge acquired in studying this subject allows the pilot to factor in his or her own performance and, importantly, its limitations, into risk assessments made before flying.

The ground-school exams must be passed before the pilot can achieve a licence, even if the GFT has already been successfully completed. Most of the exams are conducted using the multiple-choice system. The navigation exam usually involves planning an imaginary flight using a chart and navigation 'tools', taking into account wind speed and other weather conditions. Most people of average intelligence can pass these exams without difficulty if they take the trouble to learn and understand the subjects properly. Qualified instructors and other pilots never stop learning new aspects to these subjects and most are always willing to help out a student who is having difficulty getting to grips with a particular subject; if in doubt, ask for extra help.

Where to Get Training

Without doubt, the best way to learn to fly is via a course of training with a qualified instructor. Most national microlight associations can put potential pilots in touch with a suitably qualified instructor in their area. The rate at which a student pilot progresses depends on many factors, from the weather to the availability of the instructor and the aircraft. Some full-time instructors work within established flying schools that have more than one instructor, more than one aircraft and are based at proper airfields. These schools often have good classroom facilities, accommodation and catering on site or nearby, and can provide intensive courses for those wishing to progress quickly. The cost of flying training with these instructors is often a little more expensive, because of their overheads.

Other instructors only work part-time with one aircraft based at a local club strip. They often have waiting lists for people wishing to start training. If the aircraft needs servicing or is damaged, they may often have to stop training until it is ready again. Such instructors will often charge less than those at established flying schools but it may take longer to get qualified.

In Britain, those who are able to fly during the week, not just at weekends, and can spare the time and money to work at a fairly intensive rate, may gain a microlight pilot's licence in a fairly short time.

In most of north-west Europe the weather is a significant factor in learning to fly. Flying training should initially only be undertaken in the best weather conditions. Limited availability of the student and a run of bad weather can significantly prolong the time taken to gain a licence. For this reason, many north European microlight instructors now base themselves in Spain, France, Portugal and Africa, to take advantage of the better weather, and are followed abroad by student pilots from their home country.

How Long Will it Take? How Much Will it Cost?

The cost of microlight flying training varies widely, depending on a number of factors:

- age: generally, the older the student, the longer it takes;
- weather: particularly in northern Europe, a spell of bad weather inevitably causes delays;
- availability of student: those who can train at any time when the weather is suitable, including summer evenings, will make better progress than those who can only fly at weekends;
- availability of instructor: if the instructor has many students, each of them will be competing for time with the others;
- natural ability: the more natural ability the student has, the faster he or she will progress; and
- funds available: students working on a tight budget will only progress at the rate they can afford.

The British Microlight Private Pilot's Licence requires a minimum of 25 hours' flying training, 10 hours of which must be solo, for the pilot to have no operational restrictions. A licence with restrictions can be achieved with a minimum of 15 hours' flying training, of which 7 hours must be solo. The restrictions include not being able to carry passengers, only being able to fly in very good weather conditions and being restricted to flying within 8 nautical miles of the holder's own airfield.

Other countries have similar requirements, but the hours quoted above are the *minimum*, achieved only by the most naturally talented young students. The rest normally take a little longer, depending on the factors listed above.

When budgeting for flying training it is not unrealistic to calculate the cost of the minimum number of hours required and then add between 50 and 100 per cent of that cost, depending on how confident you are about your own ability. Hourly rates vary depending on where the instructor flies from and on overheads. In Britain, the high cost of fuel and the weather adds to the overall expense. The best advice, before committing yourself to flying training, is to go and see a few different instructors and ask about their rates. Speak to some of their students and some who have qualified and find out how much it is costing them or how much they spent in total to get their licence. Settle on the pace at which you can afford the time and money

The legendary Bob Arnold and passenger showing that they really enjoy their flying.

to train, and then decide whether to train in one place or to go abroad for better weather in order to progress more quickly.

After taking all the necessary factors into account and coming to the decision to start training, persevere and do not be deterred. Some people get their licences in a few months, others take a couple of years – and some lose heart and never get there. Every qualified microlight pilot will agree that the final reward of gaining a licence is really worth it. If you are ever in doubt, look at the smiles on the faces of microlight pilots when they have been flying.

Microlight Heroes: Eppo Numan

Dutchman Eppo Harbrink Numan has been variously described as heroic, eccentric, fanatical and mad! Born during the Second World War, he experienced microlighting for the first time in 1981, when he flew with a Belgian friend in a flexwing trike. Soon after, he came to England to buy two microlights, a single-seater and a two-seater, from Medway Microlights in Kent, and then set about learning to fly them.

Numan's flying training was eventful, to say the least. On one occasion, a less than perfect landing resulted in both him and his instructor being left hanging upside down from their straps after the aircraft had somersaulted. With enthusiasm and determination, he finally mastered the skills of flexwing flying and this led him on to a series of hair-raising and amazing adventures. One day, while flying over the island of Corsica, he was struck with idea of flying the whole world in a flexwing microlight. After landing he rushed off to buy some maps and began making some distance and fuel consumption calculations to see how such a journey might be done.

Back in Holland, his research revealed how difficult it would be to obtain all the permissions to overfly the various countries on his chosen route. He decided to start instead with the hardest part of any round-the-world trip – the Atlantic crossing. Over the next couple of years, he continued his preparations, increased his flying experience, and began to get a feel for what sort of wing and trike combination he would use. Then he was involved in a disaster that would put his plans on hold for some time.

In summer 1984, Numan was back in Corsica, taking tourists on sight-seeing flights over the island. On one of these flights, over the sea at around 1,300ft, he lifted his helmet's visor to talk to his passenger. The slipstream caught it, tore it away and sent it flying into the arc of the pusher propellor at the back of the trike. The impact of the visor on the spinning propellor shattered one of the blades. The aircraft shook violently and began to tumble, wrenching the control bar out of the pilot's hands and, completely out of control, the aircraft and its two occupants plummeted into the sea.

Against all the odds, both survived, although Numan suffered some facial and rib fractures as well as many cuts and heavy bruises; later, he would discover that he also had broken bones in this back. Checking himself out of hospital a few days later, he mustered the courage to fly again, and headed off in his single-seat flexwing over the sea. His hopes of locating and recovering the crashed two-seater were soon dashed when he realized it had sunk in deep water.

After a difficult year or so, Numan, with his indomitable spirit, had resolved to get hold of a new microlight and fly the Atlantic during 1986. In the end, it was 1989 before he was able to begin his attempt, and even then there were plenty of complications. Offers of sponsorship, so vital for such a project, proved unreliable; many so-called 'experts' told him that he would be going the 'wrong way', against prevailing winds; and, when he was finally ready to go in June 1989, the Dutch Aviation Authorities tried to prevent him taking off, believing that he had not obtained 'special permission'.

Once he had finally left the ground, all the stresses of planning the flight simply fell away

Microlight Heroes: Eppo Numan *continued*

and he was able concentrate on the task in hand. After crossing the English Channel, he flew the length of Britain to Stornaway, in the Outer Hebrides. There, bad weather forced him to wait for almost four weeks before setting out for the Faroe Islands, where he landed at Vagar Airfield after 5 hours and 45 minutes of flying. Five days later he was taking off again, heading for Iceland, where he ran into the bureaucratic 'brick wall' that would bring this attempt to an end. The Danish Aviation Authority would not give permission for him to fly over the airspace of Greenland, believing the flight to be too dangerous.

Andre Lafitte (pictured left), a French pilot who wanted to cross the Atlantic in a Mistral closed-cockpit, three-axis microlight, joined Numan in Iceland. Together, they tried to get the Danes to change their minds. After protracted negotiations at governmental level, they were told that if they could each arrange for $20,000 worth of search and rescue insurance, provide a well-equipped twin-engined chase plane to follow them, and prove they had permission to fly over Iceland, Canada and the USA, they could continue. Lafitte met these conditions first and flew on, but had to abandon his flight after 6 hours' flying over Greenland. It took Numan six weeks to make all the arrangements; the weather window had closed and he reluctantly abandoned his attempt and returned home.

To finance his first attempt, Numan had had to sell many treasured pieces of antique furniture. Planning to set out a second time, he sold his restaurant. He set off for Iceland in June 1990, to continue his journey across the Atlantic from where he had left off. After three weeks waiting for good weather, he was under way again, setting out over the Denmark Strait for Kulusuk in Greenland.

Arriving in Greenland, Numan had a huge argument with his chase-plane pilot. American Pat Epps and his brother Doug agreed to take over chase-plane duties and from then on things went pretty well, despite a few scares over navigation and some horrendous turbu-

lence. His journey continued over Greenland, on to Baffin Island and then down through Canada to the USA. On 2 August 1990, US air traffic controllers at New York, showing the aviation-friendly attitude that prevails across the USA, gave the Dutchman permission to fly around the Statue of Liberty to celebrate his Atlantic crossing.

This was not the end of the adventure, however; severe turbulence forced him to land in a federal park on Staten Island, where he was soon surrounded. Once the police heard the story of his journey, he was cleared to take off again and the next morning he completed his journey, landing at Atlantic Aviation in Teterboro.

For sheer and prolonged doggedness and determination in the face of seemingly impossible adversity, few can beat Eppo Numan. He has achieved extraordinary goals, sacrificing any ordinary way of life in the pursuit of a dream.

4 Owning and Maintaining a Microlight

One of the main attractions of microlighting is that pilots can own and fly their own aircraft, without having to be enormously wealthy. Many newcomers to the sport are unsure what sort of aircraft to buy, particularly if they are on a tight budget and cannot afford the type of aircraft that they have trained on. Most microlight flying instructors like to teach on fairly new machines, and particularly favour the more expensive four-stroke engines, which require less maintenance and are much more fuel-efficient than the cheaper two-stroke versions. These machines are often beyond the budget of the beginner, particularly just after paying for a series of lessons in order to qualify for a pilot's licence.

In some countries, it is not possible to hire a microlight from a flying club or school. Light aircraft used for public transport purposes must meet stringent manufacturing and maintenance standards, but microlights are not certificated in this way. Most microlights operate on a Permit to Fly, which does not require maintenance by licensed engineers and full certification of manufacturers. In this way, costs are kept as low as possible. You may be able to fly your instructor's aircraft solo when you are undergoing training, but as soon as you qualify for your private pilot's licence you cannot hire the aircraft to fly solo, so you will need to buy your own.

CHOOSING THE RIGHT AIRCRAFT FOR YOU

Flexwing or Three-Axis?

There are a number of factors to consider when deciding which microlight to buy. The first and most obvious question is: flexwing or three-axis?

The flexwing provides the freedom of open-cockpit flying, and is simpler and therefore generally cheaper than a three-axis machine. It can be quickly rigged and de-rigged and the trike unit and folded wing can be transported on a trailer. This means that you do not have to pay for hangar space, which can be expensive. The downsides of the flexwing are that it requires more physical strength to control and provides little protection from the elements, meaning you will have to wear a lot of warm protective clothing all year round.

The three-axis aircraft is generally more expensive to buy. It might have an open cockpit but most modern designs have closed cockpits. With a few exceptions, three-axis aircraft are not usually able to have their wings rigged and de-rigged or folded and must therefore be either hangared or parked in the open air and protected with covers. Those three-axis aircraft that can have their wings folded up – the CFM Shadow is one example – are often kept in hangar/trailers, which can be towed behind a car. The cost of such a trailer is an additional expense to be added to the budget.

Two-Stroke or Four-Stroke Engine?

The type of engine is an important decision, as it will greatly affect the purchase price and running costs of the aircraft. Increasingly, instructors are investing in four-stroke engines because they require much less maintenance and use less fuel than two-stroke engines. The four-stroke engine is generally believed to be more reliable than the two-stroke – a significant factor if you are likely to want to fly over large stretches of water, or inhospitable terrain where level fields for emergency landings are few and far between. Four-stroke engines do not need expensive two-stroke oil mixed with their gasoline fuel and do not need the frequent overhauls and de-coking procedures required by two-stroke engines. They are usually heavier than the

two-stroke and, being more complex, are much more expensive to buy. The most popular four-stroke engine for microlights is the Rotax 912.

The two-stroke engine is much cheaper to buy and lighter than the four-stroke but more expensive to run and maintain. Every time the cylinder head is lifted to inspect the piston crowns for carbon deposit build-up, a new set of gaskets is required. If you have some skills as a mechanic and are able to do this work yourself, the cost of this job is minimal. If you have to hire a mechanic or an engine servicing company to do this work, you will have additional running costs. Two-stroke engines in microlights also need to have relatively expensive high-grade oil mixed with their gasoline fuel.

How often and where are you are going to fly? If you are going to be in the air for more than a couple of hundred hours each year (the average microlight pilot in Britain flies 50 to 60 hours), and embark on long trips over water or difficult terrain, the four-

The Rotax 912 four-cylinder, four-stroke, water-cooled motor.

stroke engine is for you. You should recoup the difference in purchase cost within a couple of years through savings made on fuel, oil and maintenance. If you are going to fly the average number of hours and can do basic engine maintenance yourself, the two-stroke engine is the better option.

The real bottom line is, as always, how much you can afford. If your budget is generous, buy a four-stroke and save yourself some hassle; if it is tight, buy a two-stroke and teach yourself or go on a course to learn how to maintain it.

New or Second-Hand?

In the microlight world, it is often better to consider buying a second-hand machine. It is a sad fact that the majority of flying acci-

dents in recreational flying happen to inexperienced pilots. As the old aviators' saying goes, 'There are old pilots and bold pilots, but very few old, bold pilots.' The newly qualified pilot has been trained to fly a particular type of aircraft safely but still has a lot to learn before becoming an experienced pilot. Usually, in their first 100 hours of flying after gaining their licence, pilots are very cautious and take very few risks, flying only in good weather and not being too adventurous. With experience, they become more confident and want to explore the boundaries of their piloting abilities. It is between this point, and the time when they have amassed 200 to 300 hours of flying experience, when they are most likely to have an accident.

The author's first microlight, the evergreen Pegasus XL, powered by a Rotax 447 motor. This aircraft, bought second-hand, proved easy and relatively cheap to repair after an early accident. This second-generation British flexwing machine is easy to rig and with docile handling, and remains a popular and affordable second-hand aircraft.

The author's Pegasus Quantum 15 Supersport powered by a Rotax 503 two-cylinder, two-stroke, air-cooled motor, complete with passenger and panniers.

If you happen to have an accident at this stage, it is much better to be in a second-hand machine that has cost a modest amount to purchase and which will probably be relatively cheap to repair. It is possible to take out full hull cover insurance, but the premiums might be too high, compared with the cost of this kind of starter-level aircraft. Once you have gained a lot more experience, you can progress to a newer, state-of-the art machine, and consider taking out comprehensive insurance cover and possibly even passenger insurance in case of injury.

There is a healthy second-hand market in most microlighting countries and this is certainly the best option for the new pilot who does not have a big budget to pay for a new aircraft and all the hefty insurance premiums.

SHARED OWNERSHIP

Many microlight pilots choose to buy a share in an aircraft, rather than try to buy one for their own exclusive use. This system of ownership is particularly popular with the more expensive three-axis machines

The incredible Australian Jabiru UL, offering light aeroplane performance on a microlight budget – and you can build it yourself from a kit. Some say its performance is better than the Cessna 150 light aeroplane.

that are increasingly prominent in the microlight world. Many of these aircraft are almost indistinguishable from light aircraft and cost as much as a new luxury car.

Shared or group ownership is an attractive option, because all the indirect costs of flying – including hangar charges, maintenance, aircraft insurance, permit renewal and inspection fees – are shared too. Each pilot pays a standard monthly fee and then pays an hourly rate for actual flying. Another advantage of shared or group ownership is that the aircraft is being utilized more efficiently and not being left standing for long periods of time between flights, which is not good for the engine.

There are disadvantages to group ownership. If all the members of the group are working during the week and can only fly at weekends and evenings, availability can become a problem. Anyone taking the aircraft away from the normal base, for touring or to visit a fly-in event, for example, will have to get the agreement of all other group members. It is also important to set up the group properly, with well-organized procedures for booking time on the aircraft and the various ownership responsibilities allocated to specific group members or to one individual. If one member looks after maintenance and another looks after insurance, for example, and either one does not do the job properly, the whole group can be inconvenienced or put at risk.

It helps if group members are well known to each other and are trustworthy. Failure to pay monthly and flying fees on time can cause groups to break up. Failure to report damage to the aircraft or potential damage, such as after a heavy landing, can put subsequent users of the aircraft at risk.

Group ownership can give pilots access to an aircraft that they would not be able to fly otherwise, but the potential pitfalls must be taken into account before making a commitment.

GETTING HELP AND ADVICE BEFORE BUYING

Before deciding on a new or, particularly, on a second-hand aircraft, it is well worth taking advice.

If you are considering buying a new aircraft, think carefully how much and what sort of flying you plan to do. Discuss your ideas with your instructor and with fellow flying club members or other microlight pilots before you make your mind up. Everyone will have their own opinion but a consistent theme will come through from all the advice, from which you can make your decision. Think about after-sales support from the aircraft manufacturer. Is it hundreds of miles from where you live and will you be prepared to trailer your aircraft there if it needs major repairs? Do they supply spare parts by mail or courier?

If you are buying a second-hand aircraft, remember the old adage of 'let the buyer beware'. There are many pitfalls to buying a second-hand microlight, but they can all be avoided with a bit of care and some sound advice. The following checklist may be helpful:

- Does the aircraft have a new or very recent Permit to Fly?
- Is all its paperwork, especially the engine and airframe logbook, in order?
- Has the owner kept copies of receipts for parts and servicing?
- Is the seller the legal owner of the aircraft? Check the registration document.

- Has it been used for training? If so, are the hours high and will this cost you more money on overhauls and replacement of parts soon?
- Is there any outstanding finance on the aircraft?
- Will the owner allow your instructor to check-fly it for you?
- Has it been kept in a hangar, garaged or left outside? If the latter, check very carefully for signs of corrosion and other weather damage.
- Has it been involved in an accident? If so, was it professionally and/or properly repaired?
- Does it look well cared for and well maintained? If not, think twice.
- Is the price fair? Make comparisons with similar machines on the market.

Your instructor or national microlight governing body or club should be able to advise you on any particular aircraft you are hoping to buy. The best advice is to take your time, look at a range of options and do not buy the first aircraft you see.

BUILDING YOUR OWN AIRCRAFT

A number of pilots are now building their own microlight aircraft, either from plans or from kits. To build from plans requires a great deal of effort in sourcing materials, fabricating into aircraft parts and then assembling them, and usually requires both a well-equipped workshop and better-than-average handyman or DIY skills. In Britain, the Popular Flying Association supports homebuilders of all types of sport aircraft, including some microlights. Its members produce some superb aircraft, although many have taken years to build before their first flight. The British Microlight Aircraft Association also supports homebuilders.

The Mainair Sports' Rapier flexwing trike in kit form. This leading UK manufacturer specializes in flexwings.

A modern kit-built three-axis aircraft – the Jabiru. Almost 100 of these kits, which come in either microlight or light aeroplane versions, have been sold in the UK alone.

Kit-built aircraft are generally much simpler to put together and can save a great deal of money over the price of a manufactured aircraft. These are becoming increasingly popular, particularly for composite designs. In this sort of kit a high degree of pre-fabrication of critical structures can be done by the factory, leaving the builder to just assemble the aircraft and fit it out with instruments and avionics.

Generally, homebuilding is not the best option for the newcomer to microlighting. A good deal of knowledge and experience of microlighting are needed to make the right decision about which kit to buy, and many homebuilt projects are never finished, or require the assistance of a qualified engineer or factory to carry out work to rectify any mistakes. This can prove very expensive.

MAINTAINING YOUR AIRCRAFT AND KEEPING IT SAFE

One source of satisfaction for microlight pilots is getting to know and understand their aircraft. Carrying out your own maintenance is a good way of learning more about your machine, and reassures you, as the pilot, that it is being kept in good condition and is safe to fly. Take advice from the person who inspects your aircraft or from other more knowledgeable pilots until you become confident that you know what you are doing. Ask for help – most pilots are only too pleased to pass on lessons they have learnt themselves.

Most new aircraft come with owners' manuals and there is usually a separate manual for the engine. Make sure any second-hand machine comes with its manuals. These will explain the frequency and detail of the maintenance required to keep the aircraft safe and operating efficiently. Certain components on both the airframe and engine will be 'lifed'. This means that they need to be replaced after a period of time or after so many flying or engine running hours. For example, spark plugs should be changed on two-stroke engines every 12 to 15 hours, much more frequently than on four-stroke engines, and the wires supporting flexwings may need to be changed after so many hundred hours and replaced with new ones. Flexwing fabric coverings, also known as sails, will need to be replaced when they cannot pass a fabric strength test at the annual permit renewal inspection. Tyres and brake shoes or discs also wear out and need to be replaced from time to time.

Cleaning the aircraft regularly is also a good way of examining it in detail, and spotting potentially dangerous faults. A clean aircraft not only looks better, but is also likely to last longer and perform better. Microlights pick up a significant amount of mud and other sticky substances when flying from grass strips, particularly around the wheel fairings or spats and on the underside of the trike pod or three-axis fuselage. The extra weight means a greater fuel burn and diminished performance and could be critical if the aircraft is being flown with full fuel, and a pilot and passenger of the maximum weight. Mud could easily take you over the maximum all-up weight at take-off, which is potentially dangerous. Rust prevention is also achieved more easily if the aircraft is regularly cleaned and lubricated.

If you want to do your own engine and airframe maintenance and are not already a qualified mechanic or engineer, it is often possible to attend a course run by the engine or aircraft manufacturer, importer or a local dealer. This will teach you the best ways to carry out maintenance, what special tools you may need to buy, and where to get the spare parts and ancillaries you will need. Even if you do carry out all your own maintenance, get the engine looked at by a professional every couple of years, or at a major service point. This can prevent expensive failures if worn parts are detected before they fail, and can save the expense of replacing a whole engine or, even worse, the whole aircraft if the engine fails while you are flying and you don't manage to land in one piece!

After flying, always give your aircraft a good inspection and, if necessary, a good clean too. If you spot any damage or defects, put them right as soon as possible. If you do not check your aircraft after flying, you could be frustrated when you turn up to fly again and then discover a fault that you cannot rectify that day. It is a good idea to carry some spares of the things that need replacing most, such as spark plugs, a tyre and inner tube and spring clips or nylock nuts.

All aircraft can be damaged by exposure to the weather, but microlights are particularly vulnerable. Too much sunshine causes degradation of wing fabric and fuselage coverings and is believed to affect composite materials too. Rain allows water to seep into all the little nooks and crannies of an aircraft and allows condensation to occur in fuel systems, leading to water in fuel tanks, which can cause engine failure.

Keeping your aircraft in a cool, shaded, dry and well-ventilated environment is the best way to avoid degradation due to weather. Hangars (usually very expensive), barns, garages or sheds are the best places to keep your microlight when it is not being flown. If you do have to keep it outside, get some suitable waterproof but breathable covers for it.

Lastly, consider the security of the aircraft, as a number are stolen or vandalized each year. It is relatively easy to padlock a hangar or lock up a garage, but if the aircraft is in a fabric hangar or parked outside, consider chaining it to solid concrete blocks set into the ground, in addition to tying it down to stop the wind blowing it over. You should also consider immobilizing the engine; do not fit an engine-immobilizing system to the aircraft, however, as these are not approved on safety grounds. Your security arrangements may also have an effect on your insurance premium.

5 Gear and Gadgets

Having invested in training and buying a microlight, or a part share in one, and having found somewhere to keep it, can you get on and enjoy flying without any further expense except fuel? Sadly, no. You will need a number of essential items before being able to fly comfortably and safely – these come under the heading of 'gear'. You will also be tempted by a range of other products associated with the sport, which you may want to buy later, or add to Christmas or birthday present lists – these are 'gadgets'.

GEAR

Flying Clothing

Even if you intend to do nothing more than fly within the local area of your airfield or strip, you will need to consider what you are going to wear. As you climb out after take-off you will notice that the air usually gets colder as you gain height. Below 6,000ft, the decrease in temperature varies between 1.5–3°C for every 1,000ft of height, depending on the moisture in the air. Unsurprisingly, cold can be insidious in an open cockpit, but it can be equally problematic in a closed cockpit, unless a heating system is fitted. The cold will gradually creep up on the unwary pilot, first affecting the extremities, then gradually numbing the whole body and, finally, dulling the senses and affecting the judgement. During the winter months, when the air is often clear, still and wonderful for flying, the cold can be even more of a problem.

Any parts of the pilot exposed to the elements will also be subjected to wind chill. As the aircraft passes through the air its airspeed produces a flow of air equivalent to a windspeed of the same velocity. Flying along at 80km/h (50mph), the effect on the pilot's body is the same as that of a 80km/h wind blowing at someone standing still on the ground. On a hot summer's day, when even one layer of clothing is too warm on the ground, very soon after take-off you can feel quite cold, because of temperature loss through height and the wind-chill factor. On a fine, dry day, with an air temperature at ground level of 20°C, by the time you had climbed to 3,000ft, the air temperature would be 11°C; with a wind-chill factor of 80km/h, the temperature felt by the pilot would be around –2°C. On a winter's day, with a much lower ground temperature of 5°C, just accelerating to 80km/h without even gaining height would reduce the temperature felt to –12°C.

To prevent problems associated with the cold, most flexwing microlight pilots wear a flying suit. This should have a windproof outer shell and a layer or layers of thermal insulation underneath. It is also desirable to have a degree of waterproofing or water-resistance in the suit, in case you fly into the edge of a rain shower. A wet flexwing pilot rapidly becomes a very cold flexwing pilot. The suit should be designed, usually with full-length zips, to be put on and taken off easily over normal clothes, without the need to remove boots or shoes.

Underneath the flying suit, the best way to keep warm is by wearing lots of thin layers of clothing rather than just one or two thick ones. Remember also that you may need to look presentable when you land, particularly if you are visiting another

The author (right) and Peter Franklin still looking warm and cosy after an autumn morning's flying in Germany, thanks to the Mercury Flying Suit and a Polar Bear diving undersuit. The Mercury suit unzips from neck to ankle so that it can be removed and put on without having to take off footwear.

airfield or strip, or if you have to land away from your base to refuel or rectify a technical problem. Overheating in your flying suit or walking around in your thermal underwear should not be your only options.

Closed-cockpit microlight pilots often wear the same sort of suit as the flexwing pilot during the colder months, and a military-style Nomex flying suit or a cotton overall during the summer. Some do fly in normal street clothes, but if you want to display a set of pilot's wings and your flying club badge, a flying suit is best.

Gloves are essential and can vary in thickness according to temperature. Many flexwing pilots prefer to wear a pair of fairly thin fleece gloves so that they can retain the dexterity required to adjust instruments, handle pencils and tune radios, and use bar-mitts to provide the extra warmth needed. Bar-mitts are attached to the horizontal bar of the flexwing control frame, and the pilot can insert both hands into them, while still gripping the bar to control the aircraft.

Boots, training shoes or even 'moonboots' are all suitable forms of footwear depending on the time of year; again, the thin-layer principle applies to socks.

There are some ingenious electrical ways of keeping warm but these are not essential for every pilot; *see* Gadgets, page 75.

Helmets and Headsets

It is not compulsory in every country for a helmet to be worn when flying a flexwing microlight but most sensible pilots prefer to wear one. A visor provides protection for the eyes from the wind, makes it easier to breathe and prevents the nose running; it also helps to keep the head warm and will provide protection from impact damage in the event of a crash. Full-face helmets, as used by motorcyclists and racing drivers, are often worn, but the most popular with microlight pilots are open-face helmets. Some three-axis pilots, particularly those with open cockpits, also wear helmets when flying.

The type of helmet worn is usually related to whether or not a communications system is also used. Even if flying without a radio, most microlight pilots with two-seat aircraft have an intercom system so they can speak to their passenger or co-pilot. The headsets are either linked directly by plugging one headset lead into another or through a junction or interface box fitted to the aircraft. The user positions a boom microphone close to the mouth so that speech is clearly heard on the other headset or through the radio. Power for the headset can be provided either by rechargeable batteries incorporated into the headset, or from the aircraft's electrical system. If radio is being used, a headset system, and a helmet with visor in a flexwing, is essential.

The British-made Lynx headset and helmet system, popular throughout Europe and beyond.

The open-face helmet is most popular when wearing a headset in an open-cockpit microlight and the clear visor often has a chin-piece added at the bottom to keep the slipstream off the microphone and allow clear speech. Most closed-cockpit pilots just wear the headset without a helmet. Another advantage of the headset is that it reduces the amount of engine noise heard by the pilot and passenger, thus providing some hearing protection.

Many pilots wear woollen neck rolls or fleece or cotton balaclavas under their helmets. The neck roll helps to keep the cold and wind out when tucked into the collar of a flying suit, and the balaclava keeps the head warm and the lining on the inside of the helmet clean. If you provide a balaclava for passengers, wash it regularly, otherwise your passenger might feel nauseous before you even take off!

Rob Grimwood, Assistant Flying Instructor, kitted up for bad weather during a Barnet Flying Club expedition to France.

71

Sunglasses

As well as enhancing the image, sunglasses are essential for the pilot. When flying in sunshine, a good-quality pair of sunglasses will reduce glare, enabling you to maintain a good look-out for other aircraft. In hazy conditions, when visibility is poor, particularly when looking towards the sun, they will actually improve the visibility or the distance you can see. This is very important for navigation. A number of companies make sunglasses specifically for aviators and, while they are not usually cheap, it is worth spending a bit more money to get the right sort. Check that they do not slide off your face when you look downwards, and that they are comfortable to wear with a helmet.

Charts

If you are going to fly any further than within visual range of your base, you will need an aeronautical chart. Charts are used for flight planning before take-off and for navigation in the air, along with the compass fitted to the aircraft. Your ground-school training should teach you how to interpret the information on a chart to ensure you do not infringe controlled airspace or fly over restricted areas, both of which could get you into serious trouble. Charts are regularly updated and you should ensure you have the latest edition. In many countries, it is illegal to fly outside your airfield circuit without an up-to-date chart. They can be bought in paper form or, more popularly, laminated with a clear plastic film, which generally lasts longer.

Charts for VFR (Visual Flight Rules) use come in two scales: 1:250,000, also known as the 'quarter mil' (quarter million) and 1:500,000, known as the 'half mil' (half million). The quarter mil chart provides a higher degree of detail and makes map reading easier but it is possible to 'fly off the chart' on a cross-country flight unless you land and re-fold the chart. For this reason, many microlight pilots will buy a half mil chart, which, although it does not have as much topographical detail, covers a larger area for the same size of map fold.

Mapcases or Kneeboards

The chart is held in or on a mapcase or kneeboard. Flexwing and open-cockpit pilots generally insert the folded chart into a soft polythene and clear plastic case with Velcro around three sides. The Velcro strips are pushed together to close the case. The case is then fastened to the seated pilot's legs by means of an elastic strap passed beneath the thighs and fastened, again by Velcro, to the other side of the case. Chinagraph pencils, rulers and plotting devices can be attached to the mapcase with cord. This is particularly relevant for competition flying (*see* Chapter 7). Other useful bits of information such as radio frequencies and airfield information sheets can either be written on or inserted into the mapcase. The case is usually soft so that it cannot injure the pilot if its edge is forced into the abdomen in the event of a crash.

Closed-cockpit pilots do not have to worry about the slipstream whipping their charts away, and tend to use a kneeboard, either a single board or two or three joined together and folding. A clip holds the chart, and there are places for chinagraph pencils and pens; some also have attachments for stopwatch holders.

Tie-Downs

If you are leaving your aircraft out in the open but unattended for any length of time it is always a good idea to tie it down. Many pilots use steel 'corkscrew'-type pickets that are twisted into the ground to form an anchor to which cord or a webbing strap can be attached and then fastened to the aircraft. This sort of inexpensive tie-down system will prevent your aircraft from being

A map case containing an aviation chart being used by a flexwing pilot in flight; note also the centrally mounted compass.

blown over if the wind changes direction or strengthens while you are away. Microlight pilots who tour or camp overnight at other airfields and strips always carry some tie-downs with them.

Trailers

For pilots who keeps their aircraft at home and rig and de-rig before and after flying, a trailer is an essential piece of equipment (*see* photo on page 30). The wings on some three-axis machines can also be taken off or folded up and many of these are kept on open or in closed trailers. Trailers are used for transporting the aircraft by road; this is useful if you are forced to land away from your base by bad weather or a technical problem. Rather than wait on the ground for the weather to improve or the technical problem to be repaired, you can either return to your base by road or get someone to collect your trailer and then come to recover the aircraft.

Many trailers are sold with second-hand aircraft. They vary in cost depending on the size and complexity and can be supplied with loading ramps, winches or wing-racks. Some closed ones even come with interior lighting and folding beds.

Radios

Radios are not a legal requirement in many countries, and many microlight and light aircraft pilots do still fly 'non-radio'. In other countries, radios are mandatory in all aircraft and they are becoming increasingly popular for safety and navigation reasons even where they are not legally required.

Radios come in different shapes and sizes and at various prices, depending on their features and level of complexity and performance. They most basic type is the hand-held transceiver (transmitter and receiver) that either runs off a rechargeable battery pack or from the aircraft's electrical system. The smallest type is more than adequate for most microlight uses, as it can be fastened to the aircraft with a quick-release clip system and becomes fully functional for use in the air with a few simple connections to an antenna, a transmit (push-to-talk, or PTT) button and to the pilot and passenger's intercom or headset system.

Some hand-held radios have additional features such as VOR (VHF Omni-directional Radio Range). This navigation feature allows the pilot to tune into a known frequency being emitted from a ground beacon, get a bearing to that beacon, and then fix the aircraft's position on the chart by taking a cross bearing with another VOR beacon.

Panel-mount radios are used in the more sophisticated closed-cockpit three-axis

The ICOM IC-A3 transceiver – an example of a hand-held air-band radio transceiver. If the antenna and battery pack at the bottom are removed and the radio is plugged into an aircraft power system and antenna socket, the unit is about the same size as a pack of cigarettes.

An ICOM panel-mount transceiver with microphone attached.

machines, mounted within the instrument panel. These can have additional features such as 'standby' frequency selection, which allows a pilot to be tuned to one frequency and then change immediately to the pre-tuned standby frequency.

Many busy airfields will not accept non-radio aircraft, as they need to pass instructions to a pilot wishing to join their circuit and land, to avoid conflict with other traffic in the circuit. Radio is also very useful for receiving en route services from air traffic controllers, for listening to automatically broadcast weather information and, in the event of a serious problem in the air, for alerting emergency services. Many a pilot

has also been grateful for a radio when temporarily 'unsure of position' (lost, in other words), to obtain a position fix or a 'steer' to the intended destination.

GADGETS

GPS

The GPS (Global Positioning System) has revolutionized navigation for pilots, sailors, walkers, climbers and even motorists, providing a very accurate system of pinpointing a particular position anywhere on or above the surface of the Earth. Once the position is known, the GPS can give a microlight pilot a course to steer to another destination, can work out how fast the aircraft is moving and therefore how long it will take to reach the destination and, in some cases, can even confirm the aircraft's height.

The GPS works by tuning into or 'acquiring' at least three (or four, for height calculation) of the twenty-four or so satellites in orbit around the Earth. These satellites were originally placed in orbit for military use but have now been made accessible to civil users. Each satellite contains an atomic clock for precise timing and broadcasts position messages for the receivers on the ground (your GPS), to interpret and compute into your position.

Programming the position co-ordinates of favourite airfields or strips into a GPS makes navigation much easier. Tell the GPS receiver where you want to go and then follow the instructions it gives. You can set up a route using a number of waypoints (position fixes) if, for example, you need to fly a dog-leg route around controlled airspace. Some GPS receivers even have an internal database that can point a pilot to the nearest recognized airfield. Others can either draw a moving map on their display screens for the pilot to follow or, connected to larger screens, can produce monochrome or colour moving maps. These moving maps can display towns, roads, rivers and even the boundaries of controlled airspace. GPS databases can be updated by downloading information from a CD-ROM through a home computer.

At the bottom end of the range, GPS receivers have now been developed into small, affordable and very usable systems. The receivers are powered by batteries, which they do tend to use up quite quickly, particularly when acquiring satellites, or from the aircraft electrical system. Many microlight pilots now use GPS for navigation and they have proved invaluable on long-distance flights by pilots such as Brian

Milton, the first man to fly right around the world in a flexwing microlight.

Does the microlight pilot still need to carry a chart and compass when this wonderful piece of technology is available? Remember that GPS systems are subject to both failure and interference. From time to

A Garmin hand-held GPS receiver with an aviation database loaded showing nearest airfields as well as allowing user-defined waypoints.

76

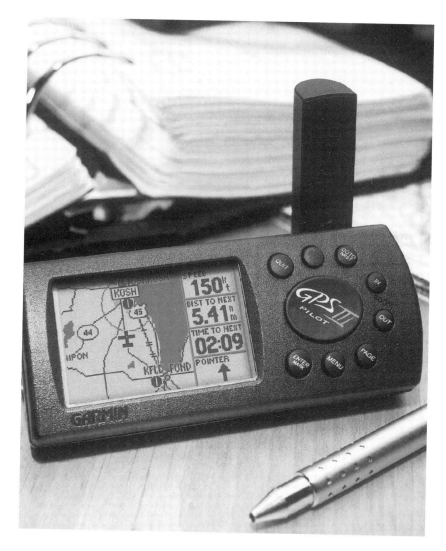

Garmin GPS receiver including a database with cities, towns, roads and railways and controlled airspace boundaries, as well as airfields.

time, the military carry out trials which involve 'jamming' GPS signals in certain areas; batteries may run out in flight or a fuse may blow on the aircraft's electrical system, and the GPS will suddenly cease to function. At certain times, satellite coverage can be poor, although with many more satellites in orbit this happens far less frequently than it used to. If the GPS is used in addition to the chart and compass, rather than instead of them, it becomes a very useful gadget indeed.

Strobes

Airliners, military aircraft of all sizes, helicopters and even light aircraft are all fitted with strobe lights, giving off flashes of intense white light at regular intervals so that the aircraft can be seen more easily, and avoided.

Strobe light systems are now available for microlights, even flexwings, and a number of pilots do fit them. They can be either fitted to the top and bottom of the fuselage, under the trike and above the wing on a flexwing machine, or on each wing tip. They are not unduly expensive and cost around the same as a hand-held radio. They do provide some additional protection against collision in the air, particularly in poor visibility and low-light weather conditions. The intensity of the light flashes is somewhat restricted by the limited power available from most microlight electrical systems. If you do fit strobes on to your aircraft, do not be lulled into a false sense of security; there is no substitute for keeping a good all-round look-out while flying.

Heated Bar Grips and Heated Clothing

If you want to fly an open-cockpit microlight all year round or around the world, you may wish to consider a little electrical assistance to keep warm. Heated bar grips are mounted on the control bar of the flexwing's A-frame and use power from the aircraft's electrical system to warm themselves up. Used together with neoprene bar-mitts (*see* page 69), to keep the airflow off the pilot's hands, they prevent the painful chilling and eventually dangerous hand numbing that cold-weather flying can cause.

Heated suit liners, waistcoats and boot liners or socks are available for those who plan to fly in very cold weather or over great distances. These 'gadgets' work on a similar principle to the electric blanket, with heating wires running throughout them, drawing power from the aircraft's electrical system.

Expert advice is required when connecting heating equipment to your aircraft. If you get it wrong, you could damage the electrical system and even start a fire.

Panniers

The flexwing microlight pilot does not have a safe, wind-free place in which to carry luggage and other useful items such as a tent and sleeping bag for touring flights, or a thermos flask of hot liquid for winter flying. Some flexwing trikes do have secure compartments for small items but the only safe way to carry a significant amount of baggage is to have properly designed panniers fitted to the trike.

Panniers are made from waterproof or resistant fabric and are securely attached to the aircraft with either webbing straps and buckles or D-rings bolted on to the airframe, or a combination of these methods. They are lightweight, not too expensive and many designs can be quickly removed from the trike and used as rucksacks if the weather is too bad for flying and local exploration is the alternative plan.

The disadvantage of panniers is that they add to the drag of the aircraft, with negative effects on speed and fuel burn. They also need to be positioned carefully so that they do not block the flow of air to any radiators or oil coolers. Most pannier sets can be quickly removed when not required or folded inside the trike 'skirt' to keep them out of the airflow.

Fuel Gauges and Computers

Many early microlight designs used metal fuel tanks with an average, fairly limited fuel capacity of 24 litres. Pilots used time and a known rate of fuel burn as the means of working out how much fuel and, thus, how much flying endurance, they had left. Other metal tanks had clear plastic sight tubes, connected top and bottom outside the tank, allowing the pilot to see the level of fuel inside. Others, like many vintage aircraft, had a float inside the tank, with a needle-type gauge attached to it. This needle protruded through the filler cap on top of the tank and gradually retreated inside the tank as the fuel level and the float dropped.

With the advent of plastic tanks for microlights it has been possible to mould or paint a calibrated scale down the side of the tank so the level inside the tank can be seen as a

Panniers can be fitted to a flexwing (seen here below the passenger's arm), for carrying hot drinks, sandwiches and so on.

specific quantity (normally in litres now, except in the USA). When fuel tanks were behind the pilot it was not always easy to turn around in flight and look at the scale on the tank's side, so small mirrors were often used to allow the pilot to see the tank without turning around. Engine vibration and slipstream often meant that it was difficult to see the fuel levels in the

mirror and fuel gauges became increasingly popular.

Some fuel gauges were fitted in the filler caps of fuel tanks but were notoriously inaccurate and not always easy to read in flight, as the indicator needle swung to and fro. Other types used a probe and sender unit in the fuel tank to send a reading to an analogue gauge mounted on the instrument panel. While these are generally more accurate than most types of fuel gauge they are still not accurate enough for some pilots, particularly those who fly in competitions.

It is now possible to fit a digital fuel computer to a microlight. This tells the pilot how much fuel has been used, how much remains, how fast the fuel is being burnt at different power settings and when it will run out. For pilots flying limited-fuel or planning tasks in competitions (*see* Chapter 7), this sort of information is invaluable.

Many microlight manufacturers now offer fuel gauges either as standard equipment or as an optional extra. They can be purchases at a reasonable price and retro-fitted to some machines. Fuel computers are rather more expensive and should not be used as a substitute for good flight planning, which allows a reserve of fuel, to provide a safe margin for error. Fill up the fuel tank at every opportunity, as this gives many more options if you have to divert from your planned route because of weather or the headwind is greater than expected.

Flight and Engine Data and Information Systems

The continuing development of the microchip is bringing ever more sophisticated instrument systems into microlight aviation. Flexwing and three-axis machines are now being supplied with digital flight and engine-monitoring systems, which can include altimeters, engine tachometers, hour meters, temperature gauges and lots of other information, all in one digital display. Although these are still quite expensive, they compare favourably with the cost of the range of analogue instruments they can replace and use less space on the instrument panel.

There are also systems available that can be fitted to existing aircraft if their analogue instruments are removed. The only drawback with these systems is that if they become faulty and have to be removed and sent away for repair, a whole range of information is lost. If an analogue instrument becomes faulty, its neighbours are generally not affected and only one replacement needs to be made.

Microlight Heroines: Judy Leden

Judy Leden is not first and foremost a microlight pilot. Her brilliant career in airsports has been mainly in the un-powered disciplines of hang-gliding and paragliding. She has been world champion three times, twice in hang-gliding and once in paragliding. She holds the altitude world record for a hang-glider launch from a balloon at 41,000ft, has climbed mountains and volcanoes to launch herself from them in a hang-glider, was the first woman to hang-glide across the English Channel, and has captained the British hang-gliding team at a competition where every other competitor was male. She has suffered serious injuries and fought against them to become the greatest woman pilot ever in free-flying. Yet, despite all her high-profile success, Judy's own greatest moments have been when flying free in her paraglider with her husband Chris and the giant condors of South America.

Judy made a microlight flight from England to Jordan for a very special reason. In 1993 she had met Yasmin Saudi, a young Jordanian woman who was studying in London, and organizing a hang-gliding expedition in her home country. Yasmin quickly signed Judy up as expedition leader and coach. Ben Ashman, a pioneer of aerotowing hang-gliders, took his microlight along and gave Yasmin her first aerotow. The highly successful expedition came to the attention of King Hussein of Jordan, himself an accomplished and enthusiastic pilot. Judy and the rest of the team returned to England with a special affection for Jordan, and the warmth of its people and their much-loved monarch.

Later that year, Ben Ashman came to Judy with the news that 24 year old Yasmin, who had never smoked, had been diagnosed with lung cancer. Ben and Judy visited Yasmin in hospital regularly as she underwent treatment. To keep her spirits up, they gave her something to aim for beyond her illness, Ben came up with the idea of a long-distance microlight flight, with Yasmin as passenger. Judy proposed a route from England to Amman, the capital of Jordan, and Yasmin suggested that they might raise money from the flight for cancer research.

They agreed to call the venture 'Flight for Life', and planning was soon under way, obtaining clearance to fly over the different countries (with King Hussein helping to arrange passage through Turkey and Syria), sorting out sponsorship and publicizing the project. Sadly, the cancer increased its grip on Yasmin and by February 1994 it was obvious that her fight was almost over. She insisted that she wanted the Flight for Life to go ahead, even if she was no longer around to take part. Ben took her for one last flight in a microlight, and the friends said their last farewells.

Shortly after Yasmin's death, Judy and Ben made some decisions about how the Flight for Life would proceed. Each would fly a flexwing microlight with a cameraman in the passenger's seat, making a documentary of the journey. Sid Perou and Gavin Crowther and their cameras joined the project, the team began to make the thousand and one preparations and soon everything was ready. At this point, Judy suddenly began to realize what she had taken on – she was a talented and vastly experienced hang-glider and paraglider pilot, but she had only logged around 100 hours in microlights, mostly in good weather over familiar territory. The Flight for Life would send her into the unknown, over hostile terrain and open sea, with a passenger in the back, but she remained determined to honour the memory of her friend.

A crowd of supporters gathered at Blenheim Palace in Oxfordshire for the official start of the flight. The microlights, laden with crew, cameras, fuel and minimal amounts of clothing and washing kit, struggled into the air, heading for France. An easy crossing of the English Channel culminated in a damp arrival in France after passing through a cold front near the French coast. After a night drying out, the two aircraft set off again across France towards their day's goal at Nuremberg in Germany but were soon forced down by a thunderstorm – another night's stop to dry out! At Nuremberg Airport, a German supporter had arranged a media reception, and the management waived all the normal charges. After refuelling themselves and the aircraft, the pilots were held up for another hour when Judy's engine refused to start. After another overnight stop they crossed the Czech border in the rain after Ben had spent some time modifying Judy's manual engine starting system to make it easier for her to operate.

Next, a sticking foot throttle had to be 'fixed' by being disconnected, leaving Judy only the hand-operated cruise throttle to regulate the

Microlight Heroines: Judy Leden *continued*

speed of her engine. Severe wave turbulence threw them all over the sky as they battled on across the Czech Republic in drizzle and against a strong headwind. At Brno airport on the Slovak border Judy had a strong crosswind landing to contend with and could not risk taking one hand off the control bar to work the hand throttle. She had to shout instructions to her passenger, who worked the throttle from the back seat while she fought to keep the wings level for landing, and then to stop the trike being blown over while taxiing to a stop. The relief at making it on to the ground in one piece was enormous, and she immediately decided to swap aircraft with Ben, the much more experienced microlight pilot.

The next day, in good weather, the team were met at Budapest Airport by Hungarian friends, who laid on free food, accommodation and fuel, and a mechanic to fix the broken foot throttle. After a comfortable overnight stop, the team took part in Hungary's largest air show, taking off for a couple of circuits of the airfield with an escort of ten Hungarian microlights before heading south to the Romanian border. An overnight stop just inside the Hungarian border again revealed the generous hospitality of local people at a barbecue as the sun set over the airfield. The journey over the spectacular scenery of Romania – where there were few places to land safely – was dogged with engine problems caused by dirty fuel. Romanian airport officials, captivated by the

flight, refused to take money for fuel or landing fees.

The flight through Turkey crossed over the Bosporus, the 'bridge' between West and East, before arriving at the capital Ankara where, again, all charges were waived. Over the plains of central Turkey and needing fuel, they landed on a track next to a road by a garage and restaurant; they refuelled at the pumps before going into the restaurant to eat. Struggling over the Toros mountains through a pass at 6,000ft, the microlights broke out to the Mediterranean Sea and Syria, where they flew across missile bases and vast dry plains, again landing on roads to refuel before arriving at Damascus Airport. Bureaucracy reared its ugly head, as some big chief of the Syrian Aviation Authority interrogated the pilots for two hours about why they had not filed a flight plan, why they had landed on a road and why they had overflown sensitive missile bases. They explained the purpose of the flight to him and showed him a photograph of Yasmin, and he relented and gave permission for the flight to continue on into Jordan.

Arriving at last at Amman Airport in Jordan with a sticking throttle, Judy had to switch her engine off and be pushed up to the reception committee. There, the exhaustion and pent-up emotion of the flight, and the realization that they had finally made it, overcame both pilots, who burst into tears. Yasmin Saudi's flying spirit had been brought home.

6 Further Into Flying Microlights

When you have achieved your goal of gaining a Private Pilot's Licence for microlights, and got yourself an aircraft or a share in one, you are free to set out on your own or with a passenger without the constant scrutiny of an instructor. For some pilots, this brings a feeling almost of anticlimax; the effort of training and study to pass the GFT and the written exams is over and there is no one looking at your flying every time you go up and either praising your skills, or pointing out your errors. For most, however, this is what it is all about: the freedom to fly in command of an aircraft.

At this stage you will still be a little apprehensive. This is the time to start overcoming those remaining fears, gain confidence, and find other things to do with your new licence and your aircraft. Where do you go from here?

PRACTICE MAKES PERFECT

All pilots will spend some of their flying time 'bashing the circuit', even when they do not have to and can fly away from their airfield or strip. For the newly qualified pilot, it is a good way of keeping skills sharp. Practising take-offs, neat circuits and different types of approach, followed by a tidy landing, is a great way of building confidence. Even when you start to fly further afield, it is worth doing one or two extra circuits and landings every few flights. Once you are very confident at your own airfield or strip, find another field or strip near by (remember to seek permission first, if necessary), and practise.

Look for strips or runways that are shorter and more challenging than the one on which you trained and gradually develop your skills at landing on such strips. Do it gradually and don't tackle anything too difficult too early. The risk is that you will frighten yourself and damage your confidence, rather than build it up. Crosswind landings should be developed gradually and practised on a regular basis until they cease to be a big concern and become just another type of flying with which you feel comfortable. Your training will have taught you that, when an approach to landing is going wrong, it is always better to go around and start again. The old maxim that a good landing starts with a good approach remains true.

Practise your navigation on a regular basis. Honest pilots will all admit that at some stage in their flying career they have been 'geographically disoriented' or 'temporarily unsure of position' – in other words, lost! Confidence in your ability to plan a route, and then successfully fly it, opens the door to serious cross-country flying, long-distance touring and, if you want to get involved, competition flying.

Every pilot should also practise emergencies in flight and forced landings on a regular basis; both issues should always be kept in the back of the mind when flying. To the pilot who has been well taught, it is almost second nature while flying to think about what action to take if the engine fails. From before the start of the take-off run until after a successful landing, you should know exactly what you will do if it all goes quiet.

On take-off, emergency action might range from landing straight ahead, if there is sufficient runway or strip left, to landing in an adjacent field or even turning back to your own strip, provided you have plenty of height to do so safely.

While flying in the cruise you should be mentally 'ticking off' possible sites for a forced landing and noting the wind direction at ground level. This way, you will be absolutely prepared for solving the problem

of an engine failure the moment it happens. When approaching to land you should always leave enough height to glide in if the engine coughs or falters, rather than creeping in over the boundary hedge or fence, using a lot of power.

Stretching your capacity to cope with less than ideal weather conditions is a useful development of your flying ability. Many instructors are cautious about letting students fly if the wind is starting to get up or if conditions are becoming bumpy, with thermals (pockets of rising warm air) starting to form – particularly if it is their aircraft (and source of income) at risk. Again, progress in this aspect of flying must be made gradually; taking off into a gale

Rob Grimwood, Brian Dowssett and Hal Curley of the Barnet Flying Club plan the next stage of their expedition to France.

will obviously end in tears for a student pilot who has only ever flown in calm conditions. Take one small step at a time instead.

Regular practice of all your flying and aircraft-handling skills keeps you sharp and confident and gives you the ability to cope with the unexpected. It will make you a better pilot and will keep your passengers safer too.

CROSS-COUNTRY FLYING

Getting away from your own airfield and flying to another is a very satisfying exercise and brings you into contact with other pilots and their experiences. It is also a great way of seeing the local landscape from a different perspective. Going with another microlight or a small group is a good way of starting to fly cross country, until you are confident of your own planning and navigation skills – make sure you are actually practising your skills, however, and not just tagging along.

Planning your flight with a group of more experienced pilots is a good way to improve your skills, but flying in a small group in which only the lead aircraft has a chart is not a good idea. It has happened that a newly qualified pilot without a chart ended up being separated from the group, got lost and had to 'land out' short of fuel, fortunately in one piece, to be recovered by road later.

A more experienced pilot as a passenger on a cross-country flight can help with the planning before take-off and is always there with a bit of advice if things start to go wrong, or if your confidence takes a dive.

Making a fool of yourself at someone else's strip is a common experience for microlight pilots at the start of (or even later into) their flying career. A poor or misjudged approach followed by an untidy landing will result in a few good-natured jibes. One strip owner suggested that a particular pilot should pay three landing fees, after bouncing twice

while trying to land too fast in a crosswind. If the approach is wrong, go round and try again. Remember, though, that any landing that does not damage you or the aircraft is not necessarily a bad one – merely perhaps an untidy one. Practice will make your landings increasingly tidy.

FLY-INS

Fly-ins are the social side of cross-country flying. Clubs or strip owners may organize any kind of event, from a lunch-time barbecue to an evening barn or hangar dance. The event is publicized by word of mouth or by invitations to other clubs and microlight pilots via microlight magazines. Increasingly, e-mail, websites and e-groups specializing in microlight aviation are being used to publicize fly-ins. Pilots fly in from all around to meet old friends, make new friends and spend time talking about their passion, and admiring and comparing each other's aircraft. Sometimes, after a late night, the party-goers will erect tents next to their aircraft, sleep in the hangar or clubhouse or stay in local hotels.

Fly-ins are fun and sometimes involve whole formations of aircraft from one club going off to visit another. Sometimes, aerial treasure hunts or other competitions are organized, and the whole family comes along to enjoy the day or weekend.

COMPETITION FLYING

Competition flying has evolved into serious international and world championship events, where the stakes are high, the competition is fierce and the tasks are hotly contested. Competitors take part for a number of reasons; some are honing their flying skills to a very high standard, some enjoy the honour of representing their club in national competitions or their country in international competitions, while others

Hal Curley, Quantum 15, one badly erected tent and one well-erected tent!

simply want to be the best they can be, trying to win at the highest level.

There are many different facets to competition flying, requiring pilots to know everything there is to know about their aircraft's performance and capabilities. Competitors need to be able to plan flights to within seconds and work out their aircraft's fuel consumption to within centilitres. If you aspire to being 'the complete pilot', competition flying is for you.

Precision flying tasks are good spectator events too. The tasks involved are limited-distance take-offs, spot landings, limited fuel tasks and soaring tasks. The first involves taking off from within a measured distance, usually 150m (500ft); over-

running the line before getting airborne costs penalty points. Such take-offs are usually made at the start of other tasks. In spot-landing tasks, the engine is turned off at a set height and the aircraft is glided down to land within a measured box, usually 150m long; touching down on a particular mark gains maximum points.

With limited-fuel tasks, the pilot is allowed only a small amount of fuel and must predict how much of a course can be flown and how much fuel, if any, will be left at the end of the task. Once the task has been flown, the accuracy of the predictions is checked and marks or penalties are awarded. The amount of fuel left is established by siphoning off the contents of the

Anita Holmes, world champion crew member, checks the remaining fuel after a task in the author's first attempt at competition, in the UK National Championships. There was too much left and points were deducted ...

tank into a measuring jug. If there is too much fuel left, marks are deducted or the task is not scored.

Soaring tasks involve the pilot riding rising currents of air or thermals using limited fuel. This is the technique used by glider pilots to stay aloft after a cable launch or a tow behind a powered aircraft. Soaring allows you to remain in the air for as long as possible while using as little fuel as possible. The pilot who is still flying when all others have run out of fuel and landed earns the highest score.

Precision navigation tasks involve planning and then flying a route to find a number of waypoints or ground markers within a fixed time and, sometimes, with a set fuel allowance. Pilots confirm that they have flown the route they have planned by either photographing waypoints on the ground or by identifying ground markers by their shapes or numbers marked on them. Other navigation tasks might include flying on a bearing until a ground feature is identified and then turning on to another bearing, all the while identifying features on the ground from photographs provided for the task and marking them on to a chart. Marking charts and drawing new course lines on them while flying is particularly challenging for a solo flexwing pilot, who will need a specially prepared mapcase or board, with pencils, rulers and protractors firmly tied to it.

Competition flying at club level is fun and allows newcomers to learn the tricks as they go along. At national and international level it is taken extremely seriously, with a series of rules and a code of etiquette that must be rigorously obeyed if protests (and possibly even international incidents) are to be avoided!

RECORD ATTEMPTS

A number of microlight pilots enjoy the challenge of attempting to set new records – altitude records, endurance records and speed records – or to break existing ones. The only records that can be claimed are those in categories officially recognized by the Fédération Aéronautique Internationale, the world governing body for aeronautical sporting matters. These are laid out in their Sporting Code and defined in different sections according to the class of aircraft. Microlight records are covered under the FAI Sporting Code for Microlights.

Altitude records involve climbing a microlight as high as it and the pilot can go. Attempts must be made outside the Airway, the controlled airspace where passenger jets fly, for reasons of safety and efficiency. A passenger jet pilot does *not* want to see a microlight suddenly at the same height.

Current world altitude records, measured in metres, range from 9,720m (31,900ft) for a solo flexwing, to 6,245m (20,490ft) for a two-seat flexwing, and from 9,144m (30,010ft) for a solo three-axis to 7,143m (23,440ft) for a two-seat three-axis.

Above around 10,000ft it becomes physically necessary and a legal requirement for a pilot to breathe oxygen from a supply on the aircraft, to sustain normal human physical and mental performance. It is also necessary to prove that the required altitude has been reached. This is done by using a barograph, which is checked and sealed by accredited observers before the attempt and re-checked after landing.

Endurance records involve travelling the longest distance in a straight line without landing. The records are currently as follows: 1,369km in a single-seat three-axis; longest distance in a straight line in a single-seat three-axis with limited fuel, 250.65km; distance in a closed circuit in a single-seat three-axis without landing or with limited fuel, 805.4km and 250.65km respectively.

Other records relate to aircraft performance. In the 'Time to climb to 3,000m' category the record is 5 minutes and 40 seconds, achieved by a solo weightshift machine. A solo weightshift also has the record for 'Time to climb to 6,000m', which stands at 14 minutes and 54 seconds. The fastest speed over a straight course is 265km/h, achieved in a two-seat three-axis machine.

Setting a record involves a lot of careful planning and organization. It is essential to ensure that the record is observed by properly accredited observers, that all the necessary rules are followed, that the pilot is in possession of an FAI sporting licence and that the record claim is submitted properly. Many potential records have not been recognized because the pilots attempting them did not follow the proper procedure. This may sound excessively bureaucratic, but it does mean that records are properly set and it is very difficult, if not impossible, for false claims to be made.

Round-the-world flights have been made by British microlight pilots Brian Milton and Colin Bodill, and Dutchman Eppo Neuman has successfully crossed the Atlantic, but their flights have not set officially recognized records. The simple truth is that no category has yet been agreed by the relevant FAI committee for such flights. The hope is that a 'Round The World' record category for microlights will be agreed very soon.

AWARDS

Awards are given by various organizations for the completion of particular tasks or achievements in microlight aviation, including the FAI Colibri Awards in Bronze, Silver, Gold and Diamond, given to those who have made significant contributions to or outstanding achievements in the sport of microlighting. In Britain, the Royal Institute of Navigation also has an award scheme for Classic Navigation; this involves a series of flights over increasing distances, some to other countries and over water, using only charts and compass for navigation. Aircraft-mounted GPS systems are not permitted for pilots working towards this award!

TOURING

The microlight lends itself well to touring. Modern microlights have more space, making it possible to carry a small tent and a couple of sleeping bags and set off on a touring holiday. The microlight aircraft's ability to land and take off from fields and small strips mean it is possible to tour without having to use large airfields, which often charge landing fees. Short journeys across water are possible – provided proper safety precautions are taken – avoiding the need to book ferries or pay toll charges.

Many British pilots cross the Channel between England and France each year to tour in Europe and beyond and many European pilots travel to the UK. Flying into microlight strips and airfields in other countries does require planning – in many cases, permission has to be obtained from the National Aviation Authority – but it is

always worth it. Some British microlight clubs have formed firm friendships with French clubs, with reciprocal, very sociable visits. (Do not ignore the minimum eight hours 'bottle to throttle' rule at such events and allow yourself plenty of time to recover from any hospitality before the return trip. It is illegal – and potentially very dangerous – for pilots to fly while under the influence of alcohol.)

When touring with a microlight, consider the aircraft load carefully. You can pack all your camping equipment into the aircraft and secure it carefully, so that it cannot fall out and go through the propeller in a flexwing, or jam the controls in a three-axis machine, but it will be no use if it means that you cannot carry enough fuel to cover a reasonable distance. If you fly from a short strip, remember that adding weight will affect the aircraft's take-off performance.

BECOMING A FLYING INSTRUCTOR

The old saying that 'those who can do, and those who can't, teach' could not be further from the truth in flying. Those pilots who go on to become instructors nearly always have above-average flying skills. In the military and in civil airlines, only the best pilots go on to become instructors and, while that is not always the case in microlight flying, it is a good general rule.

What makes a good flying instructor? First, the potential flying instructor needs to have a strong desire to be an instructor, in order to get through the training course and subsequent examinations. Second, his or her aircraft-handling skills and knowledge of the theory of flight, and all the other ground-school subjects, will need to be significantly above the standard required of the 'ordinary' pilot. Extensive study will be required to achieve and maintain this level of knowledge, and many hours of flying experience and practice will be necessary to develop the aircraft-handling skills.

Even the most skilled and knowledgeable pilot will not necessarily make a good instructor, however. An ability to teach those skills and knowledge to others is critical. The instructor has to be able to assess the student pilot, to understand the student's strengths and weaknesses and to find ways to overcome them. The ability to build the correct relationship with each individual student is also very important. Some will respond to a no-nonsense disciplinarian approach, where the instructor gives clear instructions and the student follows them exactly as briefed.

Geoff Weighell, full-time flexwing instructor and chairman of the UK CAA's Panel of Microlight Examiners.

Others will want to have a dialogue with the instructor as training progresses, both to get constant reassurance and to bring their own ideas into the training environment. Achieving the correct balance between the two styles of relationship is crucial to the way the student progresses in training.

A good microlight flying instructor will need a number of personal qualities, including calmness, patience, good interpersonal skills, determination, above-average flying skills and the ability to explain and teach a skill, and impart knowledge.

Few instructors become wealthy from their work; indeed, many can only instruct part-time because they have to keep a 'day job' in order to support themselves. The rewards of being a flying instructor are much more than financial. Being outdoors has to be one of the main attractions. Being paid to go flying is another. But job satisfaction for most instructors really comes when students experience that sense of achievement on landing after their first solo or passing their General Flying Test.

The requirements for becoming a flying instructor differ from country to country, but follow the same general path. Flying instruction usually requires a commercial licence in the UK, but an exemption has been granted to allow flight instruction for microlights. There is normally a minimum experience level, measured in hours flown and not normally less than 100, an entrance exam and flying test, followed by training to become an assistant flying instructor and then a period of supervision by a 'qualified' flying instructor before upgrading to that standard.

If you love flying, and want to help others share your passion, becoming an instructor is a good way to earn some or all of your living. It is a vocation, however, and not just a job. The rewards are usually less tangible than money but it can provide real personal satisfaction.

FLYING FOR THE DISABLED

Many microlight pilots have become involved in flying for the disabled, either as instructors or as helpers. Some types of microlight aircraft are easily adapted for pilots with disabilities and a number of charities have been set up to encourage and provide financial support to help disabled people to fly.

Benefiting from control-system adaptations that allow full control of the aircraft by pilots who do not have the use of both arms and legs, the disabled pilot is on equal terms with any other pilot when in the air. Many progress much further from simply experiencing flight in a microlight, to qualifying as microlight pilots or as instructors. One regular and highly successful member of the British microlight team has no use of his legs, but in the air he is both a formidable pilot and competitor.

Able-bodied pilots can gain a great deal of personal satisfaction from helping disabled people to experience and enjoy the freedom of flight in microlights and other aircraft. Both parties have much to learn from each other before the challenges can be overcome.

AERIAL TOWING

Microlights can also be used for the aerial towing of hang-gliders and small gliders and, in some countries, of advertising banners. A three-axis machine with a tractor propeller and an engine mounted at the front of the aircraft can be easily fitted

A Pegasus Quantum flexwing towing a single-seat glider.

An ingenious tow hook fitted to the propeller shaft of a Rotax 912-engined Royal trike.

with a towing hook with a quick-release system. For the flexwing with a rear-mounted engine and a pusher propeller there are two ways of fitting a towing hook. Either a frame is built to keep two or more lines clear of the propeller; these lines then converge into a single tow rope behind the aircraft. A more functional solution is to mount a hook and quick-release system through the propeller shaft (*see* photo above).

AERIAL WORK

Microlights have many other uses, which can be described as aerial work, including crop spraying, aerial survey, aerial photography, police surveillance and banner towing. Currently, in the UK, aerial work by microlights that pays the pilot is not allowed. (In some other countries, there are no such restrictions.) The aircraft used for aerial work in the UK can only be flown by pilots with a commercial licence; sporting or recreational licences are not considered sufficient. This is a shame, because modern microlights are less weather-sensitive than their predecessors, and are able to carry out a number of roles in less than ideal flying conditions. The relatively low cost of

The Royal trike, a German design using the popular Rotax 912 four-stroke engine.

operating a microlight, when compared with the costs of a light aircraft or a helicopter, makes it an even more attractive proposition.

Microlights are also forbidden from carrying fare-paying passengers – a sensible restriction, because microlight aircraft are not subject to the same stringent standards of airworthiness required of public transport aircraft.

A French Agriplane Condor at work over a landscape reminiscent of a Van Gogh painting.

Microlight Heroes: Brian Milton

Brian Milton is a journalist and an adventurer whose exploits have amazed and intrigued both pilots and non-flyers.

In 1969, he left England in a 1937 Austin Ruby, heading for South Africa, where he was to be married. After 2,000 miles of running on three cylinders and 900 miles without brakes, he was forced to abandon the car in the Congo when it finally fell to pieces. After all that, he was expelled from South Africa and the wedding had to be re-arranged in England.

Milton was an early convert to the sport of hang-gliding in the UK, and in 1978 nearly had the dubious honour of having his death shown on national television. While being filmed for a BBC documentary, his hang-glider was flipped upside down by turbulent air currents. It collapsed and he fell more than a couple of hundred feet to the ground, to land in a freshly ploughed and rain-soaked field. In the end, to everyone's surprise, he suffered just a broken right arm, severe bruising and a gashed chin, and developed a fear of heights!

In December 1987, Milton set off on his own from London to Sydney, Australia, in a tiny CFM Shadow three-axis microlight aircraft powered by a 40hp two-stroke engine, without any chase plane or ground-support team. He was not the first person to do this journey (Eve Jackson had already flown a Shadow to Australia, *see* page 47), but his trip was arguably more eventful, with a total of nine emergency landings. He was blown upside down on a Greek Island and had to glue the aircraft back together, had an engine failure at 5,000ft while climbing to cross a 1,800m (6,000ft) mountain range in Jordan, ditched into the Persian Gulf during the Iran–Iraq war adjacent to an Iranian attack on two oil tankers, and had to recover the aircraft from the sea and dry it out before he could continue. He was nearly killed when a military helicopter and its downwash got much too close for comfort. Later, when crossing Australia, he landed successfully in the midst of three lightning storms only to experience an earthquake! Fifty-nine days after setting out, he arrived in Sydney, breaking the unofficial record for the longest journey in a microlight.

In 1988, Milton set off from England on his most challenging journey so far, this time with Keith Reynolds, a microlight flying instructor from Kent, as co-pilot. They intended to fly right around the world in an open-cockpit flexwing aircraft in 80 days, inspired by Jules Verne's fictional character Phileas Fogg.

Again, the journey proved eventful. Bureaucracy prevented Reynolds from flying across Russia, and Milton was assigned a Russian navigator, 'for security reasons'. Reynolds returned home to his flying school, while Milton pressed on alone after crossing the Bering Strait between Russia and Alaska. He faced and conquered engine problems, being 'buzzed' by a hostile jet fighter, flying far out to sea over iceberg-laden waters and nearly being thrown out of the sky by atrocious weather conditions. Endless days of frustration on the ground waiting for official permission to enter certain countries, or for truly impossible weather to clear, put paid to the target of 80 days for the whole journey, but it was still achieved in 80 flying days.

Approachable, arrogant, articulate, brash, courteous, cultured, dependable, friendly, headstrong, impatient, impetuous, loyal, pugnacious, self-effacing and stubborn, Brian Milton has been described as all these things, but his determination to succeed and his sheer courage set him apart. At the same time he is still 'one of us', an extraordinary but still sometimes ordinary microlight pilot who flies a flexwing for the love of it.

7 Some Rules and Regulations

WHY ARE THERE RULES AND REGULATIONS?

It may seem strange to have rules and regulations in microlighting, a sport in which freedom is one of the most attractive aspects. Microlight pilots take to the air to get away from the frustrations of modern life. Particularly on summer public holidays, it is a real joy to fly above lines of crawling cars, knowing that you are going to reach your destination without being stuck for hours in traffic.

To be of any use, regulations must be reasonable. Those that are too difficult or too expensive to comply with will be ignored. On the other hand, if they are too lax, they will not provide the sort of protection everyone needs. Freedom to fly with the minimum rules and regulations necessary for acceptable standards of safety is the ideal situation. Interpretations of what is an acceptable standard of safety do differ from country to country and this affects the number of rules and regulations imposed upon microlight pilots. In some places, there are none at all; in others, there are so many that flying legally is nearly impossible.

There are three reasons for regulations:

- Airworthiness – ensuring that microlights are safe to fly.
- Licensing and training – ensuring that the microlight pilot is capable of flying safely.
- Safeguarding other users of the air, and those on the ground.

Airworthiness

Most countries have some form of airworthiness regulations for microlights. This involves first the formulation of a design standard to which microlights must be built, or to which they must conform if they are to be imported or built by the owner from a kit or a set of plans.

The design standard lays down performance characteristics such as low stalling speed, docile handling with no vicious stall, and strength requirements. The aircraft must be capable of easily withstanding the maximum stresses that may be imposed upon it in flight, without breaking up and crashing. Standards differ throughout the world but some countries, notably the UK and Germany, impose what are generally regarded as more stringent design standards than others.

Another aspect of airworthiness covers modifications. It is all very well making sure that a microlight is built to a safe design standard, but there then has to be some means of ensuring it does not subsequently become unsafe because of modifications or additions made by the owner, or because it has not been properly maintained. Some pilots seem to think that a microlight is always improved by the bolting on of additional equipment or gadgets.

Landing lights, which should be unnecessary, as microlights are not allowed to fly at night, are a common addition. Others fit strobe light systems to make their machines more visible to other air users. Engine and propeller changes are also popular, to increase reliability or improve performance. All such changes, unless properly assessed and, if necessary, flight-tested, could make an aircraft unsafe. In an aircraft that by definition is very light, each addition to the basic structure carries a weight penalty. If a modified aircraft is to be flown within its maximum all-up weight, the crew weight or the amount of fuel carried may need to be restricted.

Certain rules are put in place to keep microlights safe. In countries where there is regulation for microlights, either the civil aviation authorities or a national or regional club or association with delegated powers, will administer an airworthiness scheme. This will involve the approval of all new manufactured designs and kit-built aircraft, to ensure that they comply with the design standard and are safe to fly. It will also ensure that aircraft are inspected at regular intervals to ensure that they remain airworthy and that no modifications have been made without prior clearance by the airworthiness scheme administrators.

In the UK, as in many other countries, microlighting has become a well-developed sport or outdoor pursuit, with sensible regulations formulated from sound experience and amended or changed on a regular basis as the situation dictates. British microlights are operated on a Permit to Fly issued by the UK Civil Aviation Authority. Each year the aircraft is inspected and check-flown by an inspector and check pilot approved by the British Microlight Aircraft Association. The inspection is detailed and can take two to three hours to complete. The aircraft is often de-rigged or partially stripped down, so that the crucial components can be visually examined or physically tested by the inspector.

An inspector will have had to prove extensive knowledge and experience of microlight aircraft before being approved. It is easy to become too familiar with your own aircraft and to look at the same things at every pre-flight inspection. You will also get used to changes that occur gradually. The inspector's fresh pair of eyes will almost inevitably spot points that you have not seen. Indeed, most of them pride themselves on finding something the owner has missed. The inspector can also often spot potential problems as they are starting to develop, allowing them to be fixed before they become dangerous and, possibly, more costly.

Metal components that are subject to loads, and may begin to crack or deform as they get older, can be chemically tested. Wing fabric is tested for its strength and resistance to tearing by inserting a fine needle point into a section. The point is attached to a spring gauge, which is then pulled to a set force; if the fabric does not tear, it is passed fit.

Provided the aircraft passes the inspection and check flight, the Permit to Fly is revalidated and a certificate of validity is issued, to be kept with the Permit to Fly and the other aircraft documents.

Other components, such as rigging wires, can corrode or fray and will need to be replaced. Many components are 'lifed', that is, they have to be replaced automatically after a fixed number of flying hours, irrespective of whether or not they appear to be in good condition. Some manufacturers 'life' their components, feeling this is the only safe way to ensure the continuing airworthiness of their aircraft. Others, mindful of the cost of replacing components, leave it to the inspector to decide if a component is worn and needs replacing.

If a microlight is badly damaged in a crash or other incident, the pilot or owner must report this to the airworthiness administrators. The Permit to Fly is suspended or becomes invalid and the aircraft cannot legally be flown again until it has been properly repaired, either by the owner or by an authorized repairer, and inspected and check-flown. Repairs must not be done by short-cuts or improvization; the pilot's life and that of a passenger may depend on it.

It is a legal requirement for every aircraft to have a logbook. This records the number of hours the airframe has flown and the number of hours the engine has been run. Airframe and engine hours do not coincide, because engine runs on the ground and time spent taxiing to and from take-offs and landings do not count as hours flown. Also recorded in the logbook is the routine servicing carried out on the aircraft, any approved modifications, any accident damage repairs, and the inspections and check-flights carried out throughout the life of the aircraft. The aircraft or engine and airframe logbook, as it is usually known, provides a complete history of the aircraft. This is particularly useful for any subsequent owner and for an inspector examining the aircraft for the first time.

Licensing and Training

Qualification for a pilot's licence imposes on a student certain requirements of flying and ground-school training. How are those requirements determined, and why?

A pilot's licence proves that the holder has undergone enough training to reach the required standard of proficiency in handling the aircraft, and has the minimum amount of related knowledge to be able to make the correct decisions that allow a pilot to fly safely in command of an aircraft. The student follows a training syllabus and demonstrates proficiency in a series of written and practical exams. Who decides on the syllabus and designs the tests?

Systems do vary, but many countries use a model similar to that used in the UK, where the Civil Aviation Authority issues microlight and other pilot's licences and approves the syllabuses for flying training and ground school, and the required examinations and tests. The rationale is that students *must be taught* what they *must know*. They might also be taught what they *should* know and any additional information picked up during training is a bonus. It is an accepted principle that no qualifying pilot knows everything, just enough to start them off safely. Good pilots continue to learn throughout their flying career; those who think they know it all will usually find at some stage to their cost that this is not the case.

To make decisions about knowledge and skill requirements, and the minimum amount of flying training time needed for qualification, the UK CAA appoints a Microlight Panel of Examiners. This group oversees the training and re-validation of microlight flying instructors, carries out general flying tests (GFTs) and administers the ground-school exams for student pilots. They set the flying training syllabus, establish the GFT content and write the ground-school examination papers. CAA training standards personnel sit on the panel to represent the regulatory authority, which finally approves the syllabus and the exams.

In addition, the BMAA forms a training committee made up of experienced microlight flying instructors and chaired by a member of the Panel of Examiners. Training matters are discussed by this committee and their decisions and any subsequent action points are passed on to the Panel of Examiners. The panel then discusses these points and decides what changes or additions need to be made to the syllabus, the GFT or the exams.

This system has been developed over a period of almost twenty years. It has a sound base in experience and common sense, putting much of the control of the training and licensing procedures into the hands of those who fly microlights on a day-to-day basis.

Safeguarding Others

Flying a microlight is a freedom, which comes with certain responsibilities. If its enjoyment impacts adversely on the freedoms, enjoyment or safety of others, it risks being curtailed by the authorities.

In the early days of microlighting, when there were few rules, many pilots experimented with new designs, some more airworthy then others. Some people who had little or no knowledge of the principles of flight attempted to teach themselves to fly. All too often, the result was an accident leading to serious injury or death. Governments decided that, for the safety of potential pilots and members of the general public, microlighting should be regulated.

Today, a number of rules govern the use of airspace. These must be observed if the microlight pilot is not to become a danger to himself or others, and are either covered by legislation or by a set of rules known as 'The Rules of the Air'.

The rules cover a whole range of issues, from not being allowed to fly into controlled airspace without permission, and without being able to maintain radio contact with an air traffic controller, to laying down which of two aircraft on a converging course should give way to the other. In many countries, microlights are not allowed to fly over built-up areas, because their engines are not subjected to the same strict certification criteria and testing as the engines of larger aircraft. Microlight engines are assumed to be more prone to failure and the authorities prefer to keep the aircraft over open country, away from towns and cities.

Forbidding microlights to fly closer than 500ft horizontally or vertically to any person, vessel or structure is another rule intended to safeguard the general public.

(This can make it difficult to practise forced landings, but every microlight pilot must make efforts to perfect this skill, just in case of engine failure.) In some countries, microlights are not allowed to fly more than a few miles from their take-off point and may not fly above a few hundred feet – clearly absurd, given that microlights have successfully circumnavigated the globe. Such restrictive regulations are the result of a lack of understanding on the part of some authorities.

Many of the rules relating to aircraft have their origin in the rules of the sea. The conventions of giving way to an aircraft on the right, and using red and green navigation lights on the port and starboard wing tips of aircraft, come straight from shipping. Microlights are generally not allowed to fly at night and so do not need such navigation lights.

The rules and regulations governing microlighting are covered in detail during the student pilot's ground-school lessons, and in many excellent books. In countries where the microlighting community has a strong and well-resourced national association or club, representing the interest of member pilots, regulation tends to impinge less on the freedom of individual pilots to enjoy their sport.

THE BRITISH MICROLIGHT AIRCRAFT ASSOCIATION

The British Microlight Aircraft Association, or BMAA, has an equivalent organization in many other countries. It looks after the interests of its members by providing representatives who sit on programmes involved with general aviation, air traffic, flight safety, and human-incident reporting, and on technical committees and groups. It also provides representatives to the European and international committees and groups concerned with the airsports of microlighting, hang-gliding and paragliding, ballooning, gyroplanes and gliding.

By providing representatives to such bodies, the BMAA can present a coherent, expert and reasoned view of microlighting to the media and to those who make the rules. It can also help to influence decisions made by lawmakers to the benefit of its members. Increasingly, the Civil Aviation Authority in the UK is attempting to delegate authority for the control of microlighting and other airsports to associations such as the BMAA. The regulation of an ever-increasing amount of commercial airline traffic, and working with other national authorities towards the harmonization of different national systems of regulating and controlling commercial aviation, takes up much CAA time and money. Little of the budget is left over for looking after sport flying.

BMAA members pay a modest annual membership fee. They receive a regular magazine with articles on the sport, flight-tests on new aircraft, reports on events and competitions, advertisements for new and used aircraft and all the gear and gadgets that go with the sport. The magazine also keeps them informed of political and legal developments that affect the sport, and of the activities of their representatives on the various groups and committees.

Membership of the BMAA provides access to the network of inspectors and check pilots who can carry out the necessary annual inspection and check-flight of microlight aircraft. The services are offered at a fraction of the cost that would be incurred if the CAA had to do the work. The technical staff employed by the association can also offer airworthiness approval for homebuilt aircraft assembled from kits or built from plans, and for modifications to aircraft.

Members can ask for help and advice on a whole range of subjects, from medical certificates, where to go for training, what they can and cannot do legally with their aircraft, how they can get insurance for themselves and their aircraft, and many more topics.

National microlighting associations or clubs provide a clear and united voice for microlight pilots, and play an important role in safeguarding and developing the sport. They can also provide a basis for international friendship and co-operation between microlight pilots of different countries. For example, British pilots can tour Europe making contact with foreign clubs and airfields they wish to visit through the national associations of each country. In the future, it may be possible for most of the required paperwork and permissions to be handled, and made simpler, by national associations rather than by civil aviation authorities.

National associations also represent the interests of competition flyers, making sure that they are invited to compete in European, world and other international championships and that the rules that govern such competitions are fair to all competitors. The national associations also select the pilots and navigators that will represent their country in international competitions and make the arrangements for their transport to and administration during such events.

Whether there are five or 5,000 microlight pilots in a country, their interests will always be best served if they have an association to speak for them, whether it consists of one volunteer, or a team of professional staff supported by expert volunteers.

Microlight Heroes: Colin Bodill

Colin Bodill was born in 1951 in Nottingham, England. He began his flying career with hang-gliding and was involved in the testing and design of the first microlight models to be produced in the UK. In 2000, he became the first person to achieve a solo circumnavigation of the world in a microlight, a truly awesome and outstanding achievement.

Bodill has been a regular and formidable competitor in both national and international events in the weightshift (flexwing) category. He has been the class winner of the Round Britain Rally, a demanding test of flight planning, navigation and endurance, three times. He was British Microlight Champion in 1996 and went on to become World Champion in 1997, also winning a Gold Medal at the first-ever World Air Games in Turkey. He is one of only seven people to have been awarded sport aviation's highest award, the FAI Diamond Colibri. A professional microlight instructor, he has also passed his knowledge on to numerous students.

In 1998, Bodill made the first flexwing microlight journey from London to Sydney in a Mainair Blade with a Rotax 912 four-stroke engine, setting a new open-cockpit aircraft record into the bargain. He flew a microlight at the RAF Woodford Air Show in 1998, the first time a flexwing microlight had ever participated in a full-blown air show. There, he met Jennifer Murray, who was to become a key figure in his round-the-world endeavour. In 1999, Carlton Television filmed Bodill while he was taking part in the Land's End to John o' Groats race, from the southernmost tip to the northernmost tip of Britain.

In 2000, Colin Bodill and the remarkable Jennifer Murray were ready for the 'NOW Challenge'. Bodill was to fly solo around the

Microlight Heroes: Colin Bodill *continued*

world in a flexwing microlight, while Jennifer Murray, who was to celebrate her sixtieth birthday in the same year, would do the same trip solo in a helicopter. The two pilots were supported by another helicopter and a chase plane. NOW is the acronym for Network of the World, a newly launched media company, which set up an Internet website allowing people all over the world to keep in touch with the progress of the two aviators.

Bodill experienced some heart-stopping moments during his epic journey, from severe storms over Vietnam that threatened to suck his tiny aircraft in and spit it out again, to an engine failure in the USA where the only possible landing place was in a schoolyard. He flew at heights of up to 17,000ft to try and avoid bad weather and had to make an unplanned landing in a rice paddy field just outside the small city of Zhan Jiang in southern China. There, he was promptly arrested and thrown into jail by military authorities. By the time the diplomatic niceties had been sorted out and clearance to proceed had been granted, the pilot's demeanour had completely won over his Chinese captors, and he had become a hero to thousands of people in the region.

Permission to enter Russia delayed for over two weeks, illness and injury (caused by arm-wrestling with Russians), engine problems caused by having to run on a lean fuel/air mixture to manage the legs of up to fourteen hours' flying in a day – all pushed Colin Bodill to his limits. Then, before the final critical and highly dangerous phase of the flight – the crossing of the frozen waters between Alaska, Greenland, Iceland and the UK – it seemed that the weather would cause the challenge to fall at the last hurdle. Delays and hold-ups en route had taken the pilots beyond the season during which it was possible for aviators to fly in this difficult area. Many thought that the pilots would be forced to wait until the next year, but fortune favoured the bold and a small window of good weather allowed them to enjoy a spectacular but uneventful last leg.

Ninety-nine days after his departure, Colin Bodill arrived back in England at the historic aviation site of Brooklands. Strong crosswinds and turbulence from the trees and buildings near to the touchdown point made his landing one of the most challenging of the entire circumnavigation, but he handled it with aplomb. He was equally calm in the face of the media attention that followed his successful homecoming, dealing with television and press interviews with confidence and a sense of humour.

The epic adventure of the NOW Challenge resulted in records for two remarkable people, and also raised over $100,000 for Operation Smile, an international medical organization that provides reconstructive facial surgery for children with deformities. Since his return, Colin Bodill has been completing training for a helicopter pilot's licence and plans to work with helicopters in the future as well as teaching people to fly microlights.

8 Microlighting Into the Future

For better or for worse, depending on your point of view, the world of microlighting does not stand still. Developments in materials, mechanical engineering, electronic and computer technology all have an impact on the sport. Social, political, economic and environmental factors are also resulting in changes and, like technology, will influence the way microlighting develops in the future.

TECHNOLOGY

One of the major causes of change has been the acceptance by the Fédération Aéronautique Internationale (FAI) of an international definition of the microlight as an aircraft with a maximum take-off weight of 450kg (990lb), as well as other criteria. In many countries, development had slowed, because the earlier limit of 390kg (860lb) had been almost fully exploited with the technologies available. The 450kg weight limit allowed the design and development of three-axis microlight aircraft using advanced composite technology, to give hugely increased performance characteristics. It also allowed some of the more conventional tube and fabric designs that had been just outside the microlight criteria, and were thus classed as light aircraft, to be re-classified as microlights.

The newer designs have made use of a range of lightweight two- and four-stroke engines, developed specifically for light aviation use, and increasingly reliable,

economical and environmentally friendly. Electronic engine-monitoring and management systems, fuel-flow computers, and other electronic instruments and navigation systems are also being introduced into microlight aircraft design.

These advanced airframes, engines and cockpit systems might appear to be entirely for the good of the sport, but they have their disadvantages too. The first of these is cost. Microlight aviation is essentially about simple and cheap flying. As the cost of new machines rises, because of the cost of making advanced composite structures and more powerful and reliable engines, the ability to buy a new microlight will move out of the reach of the average flyer. As the price of new aircraft goes up, so does the residual value of second-hand aircraft and this will gradually feed into the market as a whole. Once the existing fleet of first- and second-generation microlights, still relatively cheap to buy and maintain, have gone beyond their safe operating lives, the average cost of a second-hand microlight will increase accordingly.

The second downside to the new developments is a result of the speed and complexity of new designs. Some of the composite three-axis microlight aircraft have performance characteristics that equal or exceed those of the small two-seat light aircraft used for the basic training of private pilots and those who go on to gain professional licences. While this is good news for the companies that build and

The future of microlighting? This German FK9 three-axis machine is one example of where the 450kg limit has taken microlight development. Some think that one day all microlights will look like this; others believe that the more flexible weightshift flexwings will remain popular.

market such aircraft, it is increasingly blurring the distinction between the micro-light and the light aeroplane, and the training requirements for both. Some think that this may eventually result in the abolition of a separate microlight pilot's licence in countries where they currently exist, with just one private pilot's licence covering all recreational powered flying. Others feel it may split the microlight move-ment, with flexwing pilots going their own way and three-axis pilots joining their light-aeroplane colleagues to form other associations.

This has already happened to some extent in Germany, where the flexwing is very much in the minority among microlights, and the three-axis machine is seen as the future. In the UK, the flexwing remains in the majority, but in years to come the balance could shift in favour of the three-axis machine.

In microlighting, flexwing design ad-vances have slowed in recent years, but some exciting new designs have emerged in hang-gliding. These have included 'topless' wings, where there are no kingpost and leach and luff lines above the wing, and semi-rigid wings, which have included fabric flaps that can be extended from inside the trailing edges of the wings. These wing developments are beginning to find their way into foot-launched microlights and might soon appear in trike wing designs too. If they do, the trike may maintain its current popularity well into the future.

Another idea in the UK to counter the increasing cost and complexity of microlight development is a 'back to basics' approach, returning to a simple single-seat light-weight flexwing design that could perhaps be de-regulated if it were to remain below a specified maximum all-up weight of 200kg (440lb). If this idea is accepted by the UK CAA, it could encourage development without all the costs normally incurred in getting type approval to produce either a manufactured or kit-built machine of simple construction, modest performance and low cost. Such a machine would be ideal for the pilot who simply wants to enjoy gentle flying in the local area, and then pack the aircraft up and take it home to keep in a garage or garden shed.

SOCIAL, POLITICAL AND ECONOMIC FACTORS

Social, political and economic factors have affected microlighting since the early days and continue to do so. As the costs of micro-lighting have gone up, so has the average age of microlight pilots. It is a matter for some concern that young people rarely have either the time or the money to spare to train for a microlight pilot's licence and to buy their own aircraft. Student pilots today tend to be in their forties or fifties, with grown-up children and a reduced financial burden. Such people may have wanted to learn to fly for years but may not have had the time or the money. Many complete their training and buy top-of-the-range aircraft, intending to go on flying well into old age.

Because of their financial situation, younger people are increasingly attracted to foot-launched microlights (FLMs), as are hang-glider and paraglider pilots who prefer to fly from any piece of level ground they can get permission to use, rather than having to trek to a hilly launch site.

The inception of the Joint Airworthiness Authority (JAA), headquartered in the Netherlands, has also had an impact on microlighting, although this was not the intention. The JAA is attempting to harmo-nize or standardize all aspects of commer-cial aviation throughout Europe, and beyond. It has already devised a new Joint Airworthiness Requirement Flight Crew Licensing (JAR-FCL) Private Pilot's Licence that will be used by all member states. This licence has increased medical requirements and imposed more stringent revalidation requirements than the old UK National Private Pilot's Licence (PPL) it has replaced. Holders of the old UK licence must comply with the new medical and revalidation requirements and the effect has been to increase the cost of keeping a PPL current. Changes to the maintenance requirements for light aircraft have also been introduced and this has again raised the cost of light aviation in JAA member states.

Faced with rising costs, many light-aero-plane pilots have moved over to micro-lighting, appreciating the vastly improved performance of microlight aircraft. These pilots tend to have a higher level of dispos-able income than the traditional microlight pilot and this will have the effect of driving microlighting 'upmarket'. Microlighting needs new low-cost, simple, entry-level microlight aircraft to be produced to 'anchor' the lower end of the market.

The projected increases in airline traffic over the next two decades will also have an impact on microlighting. In countries where population density requires a number of major airports to be close to the centres of population, to serve the needs of business and holiday travellers, pressure on con-trolled airspace will increase. The aviation authorities may then be persuaded by commercial pressures from the airlines to increase the amount of controlled airspace surrounding major airports. This will

The Doodlebug FLM; the power unit and harness are supplied by Flylight Ltd, and can be mated with a number of hang-glider wings.

reduce the amount of open airspace available for recreational aviation. While microlights can get permission to fly in some classes of controlled airspace, provided they are equipped with radio, the likelihood is that, as this airspace gets busier and busier, commercial concerns will be given priority. Microlight and other relatively slow-moving aircraft may be squeezed out.

One alternative would be for microlights to be equipped with the sort of terrain and collision avoidance systems (TCAS) that are beginning to emerge in airliners. One day, these systems may reduce the need for controlled airspace, enabling airline and other pilots to maintain separation from other air traffic themselves rather than by following the orders of air traffic controllers.

While this is theoretically possible, it remains beyond the financial reach of the microlight pilot. However, it is worth remembering that, at the start of the 1990s, Global Positioning Systems (GPS) were too large and too expensive for most recreational pilots. Ten years later, the size and cost of GPS had reduced to the point at which many pilots had begun to consider them an essential item. The same may well happen for TCAS in another ten to twenty years.

ENVIRONMENTAL FACTORS

Perhaps the biggest problem facing pilots everywhere is the environmental lobby. The exhaust emissions of aircraft are not generally seen as being as problematic as those of cars and lorries, but there is one aspect of aircraft that really raises the hackles of the environmentalist – noise. Although modern microlights are among the quietest of aircraft, there is a public perception that all aircraft are noisy.

People who live close to a major airport learn to tolerate aircraft noise, unless it regularly interrupts their sleep. In the countryside, there is much less tolerance to noise, particularly from light aircraft and microlights. Where training is taking place and aircraft are flying circuits around the airfield or strip, the constant presence of noise can drive people to mount campaigns to get airfields closed and flying stopped in their area. The microlight has come a long way since the early days of screaming lawn-mower engines, but the high pitch of a two-stroke engine is often perceived to be noisier than it actually is.

Considerate flying practices – avoiding over-flying the homes of known objectors, not allowing take-offs very early in the morning, or very late flying on summer evenings – often have to be adopted to reduce the number of complaints received. This is often the only way to prevent being stopped from flying. Clubs will benefit from having a good attitude towards public relations. Presenting a positive image of micro-lighting as a well-controlled sport enjoyed by responsible and well-trained people is the best way of appeasing noise protestors. Inviting local people to visit the airfield or strip can be effective, if the visit is managed well; perhaps you can even persuade them to come for a flight with you. Protestors often think that pilots are either spoilt rich people or airborne hooligans, who could not care less about the feelings of others. Show them that you take as many measures as you can to reduce the impact of your flying on others' lives, and try to get them to understand what you get out of flying.

One microlight flying club constantly received complaints from a man who lived at the edge of its airfield. When he was invited to visit the club, he told them that he did not really object to their flying, but that his wife felt that some pilots were deliberately flying over their garden, where she often sunbathed in the nude. He was taken up for a flight and realized that it was almost impossible for microlight pilots taking off or approaching to land to see his wife in the garden, let alone determine what she was wearing. In the end, he became a friend of the club and would keep an eye out for vandals and other mischief-makers around the clubhouse caravan. Many other flying clubs have gained positive local publicity by raising money for charity during social events.

The continuing development of quieter, more fuel-efficient engines, which use fuels that do not produce harmful emissions, can only also help to minimize the pressures on recreational flying from the environmental lobby and from noise objectors.

Whatever the future may hold for the sport of microlighting, as long as there are ordinary people who dream of taking to the air as pilots of their own aircraft, it will continue. The unstoppable march of technology will bring new and exciting developments. It may also solve some of the problems that will have to be faced in the future – one major challenge is the balancing of the safe operation of commercial aviation in increasingly busy airspace with the needs of private aviation. Most importantly, the private pilot must be allowed to continue to enjoy the freedom of the skies.

Further Information

USEFUL ADDRESSES

The following organizations have details of clubs, manufacturers, airfields, schools and associations in English.

For all countries: Fédération Aéronautique Internationale; *www.fai.org*

UK: British Microlight Aircraft Association; *www.bmaa.org*
USA: United States Ultralight Association; *www.usua.com*

Australia: Australian Ultralight Federation; *www.auf.asn.au*
France: Fédération Française de Planeur Ultra-Leger Motorisé; *www.interpc.fr/ffplum/*
Germany: Deutsche Aero Club (3 Axis); *http://deac.org/de.ac*
Germany: Deutsche Ultraleicht Verband (Trikes); *www.dulv.de*
Italy: Italian Ultralights; *www.ulm.it*
Lithuania: Flexwing Association; *www.deltapilot/lt/english.htm*
Slovenia: Slovenian Microlights; *www.slo-microlights.aeroklub-prlek.sl*
South Africa: South African Ultralight Federation; *www.otto.co.za/micro*

FURTHER READING

Cosgrove, Brian, *The Microlight Pilot's Handbook* (Airlife): a study guide for UK trainee pilots.
Leden, Judy, *Flying with Condors* (Orion): an inspiring autobiography.
Milton, Brian, *The Dalgety Flyer* (Bloomsbury): a tale of derring-do from a great adventurer.
Milton, Brian, *Global Flyer* (Mainstream): around the world in 80 flying days.
Rutland, Kevin, *Flying with Angels* (Airlife): adventures in microlights.
Somerville-Large, Peter, *Skying* (Hamish Hamilton): a philosophical journey and travelogue with a microlight.

Index